SpringerBriefs in Cybersecurity

Editor-in-Chief

Sandro Gaycken, Digital Society Institute, European School of Management and Technology (ESMT), Stuttgart, Baden-Württemberg, Germany

Series Editors

Sylvia Kierkegaard, International Association of IT Lawyers, Highfield, Southampton, UK
John Mallery, Computer Science and Artificial Intelligence, Massachusetts Institute of Technology, Cambridge, MA, USA
Steven J. Murdoch, University College London, London, UK
Kenneth Geers, Taras Shevchenko University, Kyiv, Kievs'ka, Ukraine
Michael Kasper, Department of Cyber-Physical Systems Security, Fraunhofer Institute SIT, Darmstadt, Hessen, Germany

Cybersecurity is a difficult and complex field. The technical, political and legal questions surrounding it are complicated, often stretching a spectrum of diverse technologies, varying legal bodies, different political ideas and responsibilities. Cybersecurity is intrinsically interdisciplinary, and most activities in one field immediately affect the others. Technologies and techniques, strategies and tactics, motives and ideologies, rules and laws, institutions and industries, power and money – all of these topics have a role to play in cybersecurity, and all of these are tightly interwoven.

The *SpringerBriefs in Cybersecurity* series is comprised of two types of briefs: topic- and country-specific briefs. Topic-specific briefs strive to provide a comprehensive coverage of the whole range of topics surrounding cybersecurity, combining whenever possible legal, ethical, social, political and technical issues. Authors with diverse backgrounds explain their motivation, their mindset, and their approach to the topic, to illuminate its theoretical foundations, the practical nuts and bolts and its past, present and future. Country-specific briefs cover national perceptions and strategies, with officials and national authorities explaining the background, the leading thoughts and interests behind the official statements, to foster a more informed international dialogue.

More information about this series at http://www.springer.com/series/10634

Shun-Yung Kevin Wang • Ming-Li Hsieh

Digital Robbery

ATM Hacking and Implications

Springer

Shun-Yung Kevin Wang
Department of Criminology
University of South Florida
St. Petersburg, FL, USA

Ming-Li Hsieh
Department of Criminal Justice
University of Wisconsin–Eau Claire
Eau Claire, WI, USA

Research Center for Public Opinion
and Election Studies
National Taipei University
New Taipei City, Taiwan

ISSN 2193-973X   ISSN 2193-9748 (electronic)
SpringerBriefs in Cybersecurity
ISBN 978-3-030-70705-7   ISBN 978-3-030-70706-4 (eBook)
https://doi.org/10.1007/978-3-030-70706-4

© The Author(s), under exclusive licence to Springer Nature Switzerland AG 2021
This work is subject to copyright. All rights are solely and exclusively licensed by the Publisher, whether the whole or part of the material is concerned, specifically the rights of translation, reprinting, reuse of illustrations, recitation, broadcasting, reproduction on microfilms or in any other physical way, and transmission or information storage and retrieval, electronic adaptation, computer software, or by similar or dissimilar methodology now known or hereafter developed.
The use of general descriptive names, registered names, trademarks, service marks, etc. in this publication does not imply, even in the absence of a specific statement, that such names are exempt from the relevant protective laws and regulations and therefore free for general use.
The publisher, the authors, and the editors are safe to assume that the advice and information in this book are believed to be true and accurate at the date of publication. Neither the publisher nor the authors or the editors give a warranty, expressed or implied, with respect to the material contained herein or for any errors or omissions that may have been made. The publisher remains neutral with regard to jurisdictional claims in published maps and institutional affiliations.

This Springer imprint is published by the registered company Springer Nature Switzerland AG
The registered company address is: Gewerbestrasse 11, 6330 Cham, Switzerland

Contents

1 **The Insecure Nature of Cyberspace** 1
   1.1 The Rising of Cybercrime 3
   1.2 The Changing Image of Hackers 4
   References.. 5

2 **Why Rob Banks? That's Where the Money is......Even Online!** 7
   2.1 Unpack ATM Attacks.................................... 10
      2.1.1 How Does ATM Hacking Work? 11
   References.. 13

3 **The ATM Hacking Case** 15
   3.1 Case Context—Taiwan................................... 15
      3.1.1 Modern Police in Taiwan 19
   3.2 The First Commercial Bank (FCB) ATM Hacking in Taiwan 21
      3.2.1 Computer Forensics and the FCB ATM Hacking 23
      3.2.2 Mules and Men for Money Laundering................. 27
      3.2.3 Aftermath....................................... 29
   3.3 Cases After FCB 30
   References.. 31

4 **Implications of FCB Case**................................... 33
   4.1 Implication in Policing................................... 33
   4.2 Implication in Theory.................................... 41
      4.2.1 Motivated Offenders 42
      4.2.2 Suitable Targets 43
      4.2.3 Absence of Capable Guardians 45
      4.2.4 Routine Activity Theory 2.0......................... 46
   4.3 Conclusion 49
   References.. 51

Chapter 1
The Insecure Nature of Cyberspace

Abstract This chapter first briefs the development of the Internet and the substantial growth of users in the cyberspace. Accompanied with the convenience that the Internet has brought to the general public and shaped users' daily behaviors, cyberspace has become an attractive virtual place for crime. While the type of cybercrime is diverse, the intuitive image of cyber criminals is usually hackers. "Real" hackers are equipped with computer programming ability, but they often start their cyberattacks with "social engineering."

Keywords Internet development · Cyberspace · Cybercrime · Hacker · Social engineering

"Group discussion is very valuable; group drafting is less productive"—Jon Postel (the first person assigns IP addresses at the inception of the Internet)

The Internet technology was developed in Department of Defense' DARPANet (Defense Advanced Research Project Agency Network) project in about 1970 to ensure military-grade long-distance communication. What makes the Internet relevant to the general population is its "privatization" or "commercialization" which emerged with the first web browsers in the 1990s, followed by varied "new" services like free emails offered by several major players of the time (e.g., Yahoo!, AOL). The Internet technology unprecedentedly connected people (IoP) largely through a computer equipped with a dial-up modem. Internet users can surf websites, although not much more than text, for information. In general, people were empowered by the Internet.

About the same time, computer technology advanced significantly, and personal computers (PCs) became much more affordable to middle-class families. Computers literally "shrank" from Electronic Numerical Integrator and Computer (ENIAC) weighted 30 tons in 1945 to an office box size weighted a few dozen pounds in 1990s. Continued advancement of computer technology also blurs the line between traditional input devices (e.g., keyboard, mouse, camera, scanner), output devices (e.g., monitor, CPU, motherboard), and storage devices (e.g., hard drive, RAM, CD/DVD, USB). Contemporary tablet PCs (e.g., iPad, Kindle, Surface) and smartphones combine multiple devices into a flat, light, and easy-to-carry screen. These revolutionary improvements bring enormous convenience to general users, and accessing to information and intangible assets is easier than ever in the human history.

Today, the technology behind the Internet is essentially a "network of networks" (Castells, 2002), which offers a wide array of services such as information distribution, communication, entertainment, education, business transaction, and finance. Millenniums probably watch TV shows or movies more frequently on their computers or smartphones than on TVs or in movie theaters. While many generation Z youths never have a phone line, a cell phone is definitely not "smart" enough to them because of a lack of data plan connecting to the Internet through telecommunication signals. Playing video games with friends intuitively means connected through the Internet, not necessarily sit side by side. Taking a synchronous class is likely to be interacting with instructors and classmates online, especially during COVID-19 pandemic. The way that people use Internet related technology come back to reshape their conceptualization of those user behaviors. Furthermore, the convenience and user friendly characteristic of the Internet has continued to connect with more and more personal devices (e.g., various types of PCs, smartphones/ smart watches, appliances, HVAC, televisions, security systems, pacemakers, cars) as well as the essential infrastructure (e.g., food logistics, health care, emergency services, power plants, transportation system, dams/water system, telecommunications). Gradually, Internet has transformed from connecting people to connecting devices. Connecting to the information superhighway and transmitting data has occurred more frequently without users' awareness. The Internet of Things (IoT) represents the converging trends that reflect a significant growth in the number of Internet-enabled devices and inter-connected networks (Singer & Friedman, 2014).

The above technological changes have substantially shaped human interactions, information retrieval, fact checking, and viewpoint formation in modern societies of contemporary time. Internet users increase from about half of American adults at the beginning of 21st century to the rate of nine out of ten by 2019 (Pew Research Center, 2020). Globally, Internet users has increased from 16.8% of the population in 2005 to 53.6% in 2019 (Internet Telecommunications Union, 2020). Individuals born after 1990s are "native" to the era of Internet; many instructors may have found that today's college students cannot and probably do not know how to live without the Internet! Families or even couples in love probably stare at their smartphone screens longer than look at each other when having a dinner together. Relationship engagement or break-up can be easily done in the virtual world with just an email or text message and without physical appearance.

Furthermore, the Internet has greatly influenced how people understand the world; "what people read, know and understand is all governed by what comes via their screens, and that is why the power of the companies that control access to those screens becomes critically important" (Horten, 2016: 3). Big corporations with an interest in the Internet may manipulate online information availability, and subsequent concerns about whether certain contents are blocked or filtered can have many implications not only in commercial/business activities but also public arena (e.g., political agenda, fake news, disinformation). United States 2016 presidential election is a recent example of foreign regimes that have a clear interest in influencing public opinions through the Internet, particularly on social media (DiResta et al., 2019; Howard, Ganesh, Liotsiou, Kelly, & Francois, 2019). If the powers of distributing online information are left unfettered, "corporations and states would be free to take actions that violate fundamental freedoms such as free speech and privacy rights" (Horten, 2016: 2).

Like previous major technological advancements, the impacts of the Internet on human behaviors are at both individual and group levels. The fast growth of Internet technology accompanied with massive users and often-slow response of social/legal system has left a gap for many deviances (Huang & Wang, 2009). Among them, crimes emerged in the virtual space but impact people in the physical space is concerning. However, general Internet users tend to enjoy the convenience and omit the important issues of cybercrime and cybersecurity until the emerged inter-connected networks bring substantial harms (e.g., massive data breach) and disturb daily lives (e.g., identity theft). With the above brief introduction about the origin of cyberspace and its prevalence and impacts, the following section addresses the scope of oft-omitted risks and damages that can be caused or facilitated by the cyberspace.

1.1 The Rising of Cybercrime

An extreme type of human interactions is conceptualized and legally defined as criminal conducts. The horizon of criminology has also reached a new territory of cyberspace that is constructed by inter-connected computers, devices, and machines. Social science research and law studies have demonstrated that cybercrime is a complex issue involving not just the technology but an array of social and psychological dimensions.

There are many terminology and definitions have been used to describe emerged new deviance and label crimes committed via a computing device. Earlier terms like 'computer crime' generally refer to offenders educated with special knowledge of computer technology and commit a crime whose commission involves a computer (Grabosky, 2001). Later 'Internet crime' usually means "a crime committed using an Internet-connected computer." Probably first introduced by Wall (1998, 2007), the long-lasting term is cybercrime that is generally defined as "crime that is committed or facilitated by cyberspace."

There are two basic issues in the theoretical discussion of cybercrime. First, the definitions of cybercrime suffer from the limitation of means used in criminal incidents. The most often used definition of cybercrime is "crime committed or facilitated by the cyberspace" (Wall, 2007). Using a knife, gun, rope, toxic substance, or a vehicle to kill another person does not change the core elements of murder. If we would not accuse a suspect "stone crime" when a rock is used in a murder case, why do we accept the term and definition of cybercrime in rigorous discussion in academia? Second, which is somewhat related to the first point, the typologies of cybercrime in use are not completely satisfying, and types of cybercrime are not even mutually exclusive. Further, the advancement of technology may change desirable targets—when Ford T model became more widely affordable, the theft of horse carts dropped substantially, but it does not change the nature of crime. In a similar vein, banks remain attractive places to criminals, but the targets of attack might have shifted from tellers to ATMs for the desirable cash.

While some may argued that cybercrimes are "old wine in new bottles", this book chooses to place attention on criminal hackings target bank industry, with a focus on attacks against ATMs. One high-profile case of ATM hacking is studied and analyzed, followed by a thorough discussion of implications in policing, cyber security, and theory.

1.2 The Changing Image of Hackers

To many people, the first image of cyber criminals usually is hackers. However, the meaning of "hacker" and activities constitute hacking has changed significantly from the inception of the term. At the beginning and developing stage of computer technology, hackers refer to a very small group of experts who are knowledgeable in computer sciences and passion to improve the efficiency and robustness of computers. Early hackers are motivated to discover vulnerabilities and to advance computer-related technologies, with a mindset of approaching a better human society aided by computers. Hacking is applying a set computer and network related knowledge to access information system with or without authorization, but the intention was to improve the technology. After 1980s, a series of hacking incidents and how they are covered by the mass media change the public image of hackers. In general, hackers turned into criminals with malicious intentions, and this image continued until today (Britz, 2013). Typology of hackers like "white hat" and "black hat" are used to differentiate authorized hackings (in order to test the information system) from unauthorized hackings (usually committed with self-interest or malicious intentions), but the gray area filled with "gray hat" is growing with new technology applied in the cyberspace where social interactions become much diverse and new valuable targets introduced.

In fact, there is no single definition for computer hacker in the literature or among the community of hackers. Within the arena of social science research, the discussion of hacking often focuses on hacking with malicious intent. Some techniques like guessing another person's password and/or username fall into the scope of hacking but involve no knowledge of computer and Internet technology (Chua & Holt, 2016). For instance, without coding ability, the 'homeless hacker' Adrian Lamo had used his aged laptop to exploit major companies' (e.g., Microsoft, AOL, Bank of America, WorldCom, Citicorp) networks from the West coast to the East coast of America (Kahn, 2004). Others may simply download or purchase available applications through online sources, legal or illegal. These "script kiddies" or "kidiots" also fall into the scope of hacking within behavioral and legal frameworks, although they do not write computer programming languages and may not have knowledge about how to identify or use known vulnerabilities. The above two types of hackers are more commonly studied, while malware use or creation is rare (Rogers, Smoak, & Liu, 2006). The most sophisticated group of hackers are those able to write computer codes or serve as experts of computer-related technologies and cybersecurity in the field. Some may be activists (or so called hacktivists) in the anonymous virtual world (Chua & Holt, 2016).

When "black-hat" programming-enabled hackers commit cybercrime, the damage can be enormous. In the era of Internet, hackers with criminal intentions have many ways to abuse the Internet and launch cyberattacks against financial institutions. "Denial of Service" (DoS) or "Distributed Denial of Service" (DDoS) are often used cyberattack techniques that abuse a large number of compromised computers (*zombies*) or a network of computers (*botnet*) to overwhelm the target online service. These compromised computers are infected by malware (e.g., Trojan horse or worm) to simultaneously bombard the targeted servers or information systems and "flood" the capacity of online services like e-commerce websites or email. Once these available slots of services on the targeted servers or systems are "occupied" by attackers, the system becomes unavailable to legitimate users. An analogy is that a car or ambulance cannot pass a two-lane road full of illegal parking vehicles. For example, a group of hackers named Cyber Fighter of Izz ad-Din al-Qassam had launched a series of DDoS attacks against a few U.S. banks like Wells Fargo, Bank of America, and JP Morgan and Chase, as well as other financial institutions like credit unions (Gonsalves, 2013).

Although hackers may be equipped with programming ability, they often start with "social engineering" to have their first step into the targeted information system. Social engineering refers to attackers attempt to use deceptive tactics and take advantage of victims' trust in order to obtain sensitive information or gain access privileges. For decades, social engineering remains the most often used method by hackers to take the initial step of cyberattacks (Mitnick & Simon, 2001; Schwartz, 2017). Upon the first intrusion of the information system, hackers can gradually take control of connected computers and cause much more damages.

References

Britz, M. (2013). *Computer forensics and cyber crimes: An introduction* (3rd ed.). Upper Saddle River, NJ: Pearson Education.
Castells, M. (2002). *The internet galaxy: Reflections on the internet, business, and society.* Oxford: Oxford University Press.
Chua, Y. T., & Holt, T. J. (2016). A cross-national examination of the techniques of neutralization to account for hacking behaviors. *Victims & Offenders, 11*, 534–555.
DiResta, R., Shaffer, K., Ruppel, B., Sullivan, D., Matney, R., Fox, R. et al. (2019). The tactics & tropes of the internet research agency. New Knowledge.
Gonsalves, A. (2013, April 25). Islamic group expands targets in bank DDoS attacks. Retrieved October 10, 2020, from https://www.csoonline.com/article/2133291/islamic-group-expands-targets-in-bank-ddos-attacks.html

Grabosky, P. N. (2001). Virtual criminality: Old wine in new bottles? *Social and Legal Studies, 10*, 243–249.

Horten, M. (2016). *The closing of the net.* Cambridge, UK: Polity Press.

Howard, P. N., Ganesh, B., Liotsiou, D., Kelly, J., & Francois, C. (2019). *The IRA, social media and political polarization in the United States, 2012–2018. Computational Propaganda Research Project.* Oxford: University of Oxford.

Huang, W., & Wang, S.-Y. K. (2009). Emerging cybercrime variants in the socio technical space. In B. Whitworth & Aldo de Moor (Eds.), *Handbook of research on socio-technical design and social networking systems* (pp. 209–220). IGI Global: Hershey, PA.

Internet Telecommunications Union (ITU) statistics for 2020. Retrieved from http://www.itu.int/

Kahn, J. (2004). The homeless hacker v. the New York Times. Retrieved October 10, 2020 from https://www.wired.com/2004/04/hacker-5/

Mitnick, K. D., & Simon, W. L. (2001). *The art of deception: Controlling the human element of security.* Hoboken, NJ: John Wiley & Sons.

Pew Research Center. (2020). Internet/Broadband Fact Sheet. Retrieved from https://www.pewresearch.org/internet/fact-sheet/internet-broadband/

Rogers, M., Smoak, N. D., & Liu, J. (2006). Self-reported deviant computer behavior: A big-five, moral choice, and manipulative exploitive behavior analysis. *Deviant Behavior, 27*(3), 245–268.

Schwartz, M. J. (2017, September 27). ATM hackers double down on remote malware attacks. Bank Info Security. Retrieved October 10, 2020, from https://www.bankinfosecurity.com/atm-hackers-double-down-on-remote-malware-attacks-a-10338

Singer, P. W., & Friedman, A. (2014). *Cybersecurity and cyberwar: What everyone needs to know.* New York, NY: Oxford University Press.

Wall, D. (1998). Catching cybercriminals: Policing the internet. *International Review of Law, Computers & Technology, 12*, 201–218.

Wall, D. (2007). *Cyber crime: The transformation of crime in the information age.* Polity Press.

Chapter 2
Why Rob Banks? That's Where the Money is......Even Online!

Abstract A bank is a financial institution that collects and lends money, and ATMs is one of the oft-used applied technology/machine that is attractive to potential criminals. This chapter addresses the mechanical nature of ATMs and then discusses an array of ATM attacks, ranging from those occurred in the physical space to cyberspace. Chapter Two ends with a discussion of different approaches that cyber criminals can theoretically hack into an ATM.

Keywords Bank · Fraud · Skimming · ATM attack

Phishing is a technique of social engineering that cyber criminals often use to deceive potential victims in order to gain valuable information, goods, services, or tokens. Tricked victims may reveal personal identifying information (PII), passwords, and banking data. Phishing can be carried out by different means like emails, bogus websites, pop-up windows on computer screens, phone calls, text messages to reach potential victims. Spams, unsolicited email sent in bulk, is a frequently used technique by perpetrators to spread the baits and "phish".

The contemporary information technology offers a new twist on old fraud schemes, and criminals can simply use emails to reach their targets. Unlike traditional criminals and fraudsters, contemporary means is very inexpensive—a click on keyboard can send out thousands of scam emails simultaneously with very little efforts in a very short period of time. Perhaps only a few would respond to thousands of scam emails sent, but each of those few replies can lead to thousands of dollars of gain to the perpetrators. The return of using contemporary information technology is lucrative in many aspects. Thus, the more scam emails and "diversified" types of fraud attempted, the more likely cyber criminals can successfully take advantage from a pool of nearly unlimited number of victims. There are hundreds if not thousands of frauds that criminals can choose from—identity theft, Nigerian scam/advanced-fee, steal sensitive personal information/data breach, mortgage fraud, insurance fraud, investment schemes, IRS scams, fictitious charities, work-from-home schemes—to name a few that are still in practice. Scammers cast wide nets in the ocean of cyberspace to catch what they look for or pick up those hook on baits. The classic Nigerian email scams (also called *419 fraud*) promise victims a huge amount of money with a condition of a relatively small amount of advanced fee. Perpetrators use different appealing and urgent scenarios (e.g., wealthy heirs need hurried help to move huge funds out of their countries/tribes, emotional pleas for emergency aid) to attract potential victims engaging their deceiving emails. Receivers of these email scams are asked to provide contact information and sometimes bank account details. All these information are valuable "goods" in black markets or means to take further financial advantages from the victims, including breeding further identities.

Some scams and frauds have been existed long before the era of Internet, such as identity theft and insurance scams. Criminals can "dive" into trach to find confidential information, which is supposed to be shredded, and further impersonate or cause financial damages to the victims. Frauds were committed largely via other means of communication like USPS mail and telephone. However, cyberspace offers great convenience for criminals to reach out a much large number of potential targets without physical constrains. The popularity of email service brings an incredible tool to scammers. In addition, the characteristic of anonymity online greatly lowers the risk of being caught. Collectively, "doing business online" is a rational choice for perpetrators.

Phishing messages usually are well-crafted information designed to trigger victims' emotion (e.g., greed, anxious, upset, deep desire) that intentionally calls for immediate response before the victims validating the source of information. Often, phishing messages are prepared to set a tone of hurry and negative consequences of delay or inaction. Examples like suspension of accounts and assets (e.g., bank, credit card, email, retirement fund) and threats of security (e.g., computer virus infection) are often seen scenarios. These messages usually sent through emails but can also delivered through phone text messages/SMS, applications on mobile devices, or other information services. A phishing message imitates and strives to look like it comes from an authentic organization or a reliable individual. Sometimes, to make the phishing messages look like real, organization logos or nicely crafted images are used to increase its credibility. Potential victims are informed by the phishing message that their prompt action is needed to regain their control of accounts or assets. A hyperlink leading to a bogus phishing website can be provided in the message to potential victims for a quick remedy, which actually victimizes them if clicked. Contemporary uniform resource locators (URLs) shortening, which is designed to produce shorter hyperlinks for the easiness of usage, can be abused to redirect users to malicious sites because they cannot be easily verified by viewing the content of the hyperlinks. By the time an Internet user lands on the phishing sites, malware may have automatically downloaded and installed on the victims' devices. These malware function from recording key strokes (*keyloggers*) to opening a "backdoor" (*Trojan horse*) of the computer system for remote cyber criminals. The phishing websites can also ask the victims to type in confidential information (e.g., account username and password, PIN, answers of personal security questions) in order to recover their accounts.

Usually, if general receivers carefully examine the phishing messages, there are certain characteristics appear across the board but rarely occur in authentic ones, such as writing problems (e.g., spelling errors, odd expressions), inconsistent format in the text, and low resolution or weird proportion of the graphics embedded in the message. More Internet savvy users usually can find other inconsistencies like the difference between domain of the message and the originating IP address.

However, during an uncommon time of major incidents (e.g., pandemics, terrorism attacks, earthquakes, tsunamis, large scale power outage), opportunities usually are emerged for potential fraudsters to target banks and their customers. Recent COVID-19 pandemic has led to an overall higher level of uncertainty and volatility across all groups of the general population, and US FBI has received an instant increase of complaints regarding pandemic-related frauds. A large scale of infection and spread of the coronavirus has generated a great demand and then shortage of personal protective measures. Also, the initial coping strategy of stay-in-shelter policy and subsequent economic contraction has pressed business to strive to survive. The above urgent situations create opportunities for fraudsters to take advantages from ordinary people and businesses. For instance, fraudsters have used spoofed business emails or nearly identical email addresses to redirect funds from their target victims. These funds, which are for purchasing personal protective equipment (PPE) or of paycheck protection program (PPP), are redirected from target companies' bank accounts to overseas accounts controlled by criminals. Sudden social and environmental changes loosen security checks and safety mechanisms established during normal time. Legitimate business may be asked to pay advance fee to secure their orders of short-of-supply PPE during the pandemic. Furthermore, soaring unemployment rate motivates individuals to act as money mules that transfer funds through their personal bank accounts (Shivers, 2020).

Today's online ads (e.g., banner advertisements) are rich with JavaScript, Flash, and other computer application code to engage legitimate shoppers. However, cyber criminals can misuse these features to introduce malicious codes and "sneak" into victims' devices. Once malware has been slipped onto victims' computers, their user habits and styles, especially top administrators, can be valuable information to prepare for subsequent "customized attacks." For example, the CFO of a company might receive an email, seemingly from the CEO, ordering a large amount of goods to be transferred or paid. Although consumers are not liable for fraudulent electronic transactions according to U.S. Electronic Funds Transfer Act, the borderless nature of the cyberspace has many to offer for cybercriminals who may reside in countries with loose or nonexistent laws against cybercrime. For instances, many cyber thieves set up operations in Eastern European and many telecommunication fraudsters work from African countries where laws and law enforcement for cybercrime is lax or lacked.

Cyber criminals may also abuse compromised computers or deceive victims to collect banking credentials of key personnel of the targeted institutions. These stolen credentials are then used to authorize funds transferring from the companies' bank accounts to a destination account accessible to the criminals but out of the area that law enforcement can reach. Also, these valuable credentials can be sold through underground markets, on top of being used to facilitate other data breach.

A famous apocryphal story is that Sutton was asked by reporter Mitch Ohnstad why he robbed banks. According to Ohnstad, he replied, "Because that's where the money is. (quoted from Wikipedia)

The above quote provides one of many good reasons that criminals applied different technologies to target banks across generations. As a key component of financial industry, banks function to efficiently allocate funds from savers (e.g., individuals, financial institutions, government) to borrowers. When most people and institutions in modern societies have adopted the Internet to a great extent, banks are no exception of the trend. For individuals, online banking is a convenient option to manage their assets and to finance. For financial institutions, computers and Internet technology have been adopted to facilitate asset management, security checks, funds transfer, loan/credit application and process, and investment. Prior to the era of Internet, different technologies have been employed in bank industry to provide convenient means for their customers, and automatic teller machines (ATM) is a common example.

Like any applied technology, credit cards and debit cards issued by banks, for example, not only bring convenience to customers but also offers opportunities for criminals who can take financial advantages from both customers and issuing institutions. ATM skimming is one of the popular techniques that offenders have abused to target individuals. Offenders may install a skimmer, which technologically speaking is a card reader, looks very similar to the ATM card reader in color and texture and fits right over the ATM. As customers insert their cards, account information is stored on the skimmer or sent to close-by criminals' devices. Criminals may use a keypad overlay placed on top of the ATM keypad, and PINs typed by customers are also stored on this device. Criminals can also install a hidden camera in conjunction with the other two devices to record customers typing PINs into the ATM keypad. A hidden camera may look like a light fixture nearby the screen of the ATM. Similar skimming have been found in other locations like gas pumps and restaurants where a variety of cards (e.g., credit card, debit card, gift card) can be skimmed. Actually, the more types of card that an ATM is programmed to process, the higher risk of invasion it involves.

2.1 Unpack ATM Attacks

There are many types of ATM attacks in use, ranging from sophisticated technological techniques to straightforward and labor-intense means. Offenders can haul away the ATMs, stand-alone or wall-attached, with trucks in hopes of cracking to open them later (EAST, 2019). More oft-seen attacks involve offenders installing fake card readers to steal card numbers (skimming), hide tiny surveillance cameras to capture PIN numbers, and/or cover the dispensing slot to intercept money. Such type of ATM attacks is popular internationally. For instances, India reported such cases increased more than 2.5 times between 2014 and 2016 (Mallapur, 2017), and local police still promote the awareness of skimming in the US. The most sophisticated attacks probably is abusing required knowledge of information and computer technology, as well as financial services software and networks, for offenders to hack into the targeted ATMs. The last type of attacks also clearly indicates the shift of targets from customers and their bank-issued cards to the financial institutions.

2.1.1 How Does ATM Hacking Work?

An ATM is essentially a computer with a safe. The computer connects to the bank's internal network and processing center through network devices for remote administration and software update. Additionally, the computer controls ATM's card reader, keyboard/keypad, and the safe where cash is stored and ready to dispense. Although the safe is made by robust material like steel and concrete, the controlling computer is surprisingly under-protected—manufacturers usually lock it behind a plastic door and the same lock for the same series of ATM (Rolfe, 2018). When processing a transaction on an ATM, the computer receives inputs from card reader and keypad, communicates with the bank's processing center (servers) through a wired or wireless network, and dispenses cash upon receiving a confirmed request. Intercepting any section of the entire communications can then compromise the security of the targeted ATMs, infect the ATMs with malware, obtain card information, and steal cash.

Hackers may insert a "black box"—a pre-programmed mini-computer sending fake commands—between ATM's computer and safe. This type of attacks requires hackers to be physically next to the targeted ATMs and redirect communications between the computer and the safe. As stated above, an ATM is essentially a computer that often equips with USB ports where hackers can also initiate their attacks. Thus, an USB carrying malware can be used to hack into ATMs' computer and then control the dispenser. Most ATM computers operate Microsoft windows, and any vulnerabilities of the operating system can be applied to ATMs as well. That is, any software patches are not updated timely can become vulnerabilities to the security of ATMs. Without touching the network communications between ATMs and the bank's processing center, on-site hackers can take over an ATM, primarily the computer, and dispense cash.

Hacking into ATMs through the connected network takes about 10–20 min to complete the attack (Rolfe, 2018), with all the groundwork settled. Criminals may be physically present to ATMs and interrupt the communications between the ATM and bank's processing center with an Ethernet cable connecting to the ATM. Criminals may also intercept ATMs' request of confirming transaction with an inserted "mock" bank processing center, which falsely approves the request. This type of attacks is conceptually grouped as "man-in-the-middle", which literally means that hackers intercept and manipulate communications between the targeted ATMs and the authorizing bank's process center. The authentic communications through bank's internal network are redirected and replaced with hackers' fake commands sending to the targeted ATMs.

Another type of attacks focusing on ATMs' network communications, such as equipment that ATMs use to send and receive communications through internal networks of the bank. Hackers may connect to ATM's network equipment and exploit its vulnerabilities in order to bypass or disable the security mechanisms. Modems that bridge the network communications between ATMs and the bank's servers can also be hackers' initial point of intrusion. Hacking into ATMs through network has a greater implication of potential damages, as bank's internal networks, servers, and computers managing much larger assets can be at criminals' disposal. Cyber criminals have utilized a family of malware, such as Alice, Carbanak, CutletMaker, GreenDispenser, Ploutus, Radpin, Ripper, Skimer, and Suceful, which are available on dark web markets. Since banks practically use the same configuration on a large numbers of ATMs, one successful ATM attack means dozens if not dozens of hundreds cases can be replicated (Rolfe, 2018).

In a similar vein, hacking into ATMs does not have to start with intercepting communications at the end of an ATM; hackers can initiate attacks from any other point of the bank's networks. Often, hackers use spear phishing emails to bait targeted bank personnel and to obtain their credentials of information system. These emails look like coming from legitimate sources, but they are customized to carry malware to exploit vulnerabilities of bank employees' terminals. Once the initial step successfully infects an employee's computer, further invasions can be done through connected networks internal of the bank. Digital forensic evidence shows that it takes several weeks to compromise financial institution's internal networks and infect other computers. The financial loss is significant; the magnitude of damage usually starts with a million US dollars as the basic unit. In their report, Group-IB & Fox-IT (n.d.) indicated that the total financial damage was estimated to be one billion rubles (approximately 25 million US dollars), largely occurred within the second half of 2014. Earlier cases show that victims are located in Russia, U.S., Germany, China, and Ukraine, and this type of attacks has spread to other regions like Europe and Asia (Kaspersky Lab, 2015). With more cases soaring on the surface, victimized banks scattered in Armenia, Belarus, Bulgaria, Estonia, Georgia, Kyrgyzstan, Moldova, Netherlands, Poland, Romania, Russia, Spain, Britain, and Malaysia (Finkle, 2016).

The following chapter focuses on a significant case that a financial institution's internal networks were used to dispense cash from targeted ATMs where money mules stand by to collect it. This case is significant for the only case arresting criminals and recovering the vast majority of the stolen cash within a week in an Asian setting.

References

EAST. (2019, September 4). ATM Physical Attacks in Europe on the increase. Retrieved October 10, 2020 from https://www.association-secure-transactions.eu/atm-physical-attacks-in-europe-on-the-increase/

Finkle, J. (2016, November 22). Hackers remotely steal ATM cash in latest twist on cyber bank heists. Retrieved October 10, 2020, from https://www.insurancejournal.com/news/international/2016/11/22/433017.htm

Group-IB & Fox-IT. (n.d.). Anunak: APT Against Financial Institutions.

Kaspersky Lab. (2015). Carbanak APT: The Great Bank Robbery.

Mallapur, C. (2017, November 14). ATM/Debit card fraud more than doubled over 2 years. Retrieved from https://www.factchecker.in/atmdebit-card-fraud-more-than-doubled-over-2-years/

Rolfe, A. (2018). ATM hacking report: Scenarios from 2018 ATM hacks. Payments Industry Intelligence.

Shivers, C. A. (2020, June 9). COVID-19 Fraud: Law Enforcement's Response to those Exploiting the Pandemic. Assistant Director, Criminal Investigation Division, Federal Bureau of Investigation. Statement before the Senate Judiciary Committee. Retrieved from https://www.judiciary.senate.gov/imo/media/doc/Shivers%20Testimony.pdf

Chapter 3
The ATM Hacking Case

Abstract Chapter Three unpacks an unique case of ATM hacking that occurred to the First Commercial Bank (FCB) in Taiwan. To facilitate readers' assessment of the uniqueness and generalizability of the case, Taiwan's social-historical context is introduced, followed by briefing its two major law enforcement agencies. The FCB case is thoroughly discussed, including the group actions by cyber criminals—Carbanak/Cobalt—and law enforcement agencies' responses. Multiple sources of empirical data and documents are used to portray the incident in a chronological order.

Keywords ATM hacking · First Commercial Bank · FCB · Taiwan · Democracy · National Police Agency · NPA · Ministry of Justice Investigation Bureau · MJIB · Carbanak · Cobalt

With an overview of ATM hacking, this chapter elaborates a case study of ATM hacking occurred in Taiwan. Among many incidents of sophisticated ATM hacking in the world, this case is the first one to punish criminals through the justice system. The Taiwanese police recovered the vast majority of the stolen cash, while the average loss was about two million dollars per incident for cases in Russian territory and post-Soviet space (Group-IB & Fox-IT, n.d.). Rich qualitative data of the incident, including interviews and documents, were obtained and analyzed to reconstruct the case profile and modus operandi of ATM hacking. To provide a full scope of the picture, this chapter first addresses the historical-socioeconomic context of the study site and law enforcement agencies of this democracy.

3.1 Case Context—Taiwan

Located off China's Southeastern coast, Taiwan (formerly known as Formosa) is a densely populated state—the current population is about 23 million on 13,855 square miles mountainous island. Taiwan is ethnically homogeneous (Han population), and both Mandarin and English are official languages in current democratic regime. In ancient history of Taiwan, linguistic anthropologists believe that Taiwan's diverse indigenous people are branches of the Austronesian language group that reached as far as Easter Island. After seventeenth century, many mainland immigrants, largely undocumented from today's perspective, moved from southern provinces of China, and some married indigenous Taiwanese. This island was then partially occupied by Dutch and Spain for a short period and governed by Qing Dynasty and Japan for decades. Geopolitically, Taiwan is centrally located between Japan and the Philippines and in close proximity to many of world's most important shipping lanes in west Pacific region (Phillips, 2003). The island is so geopolitically vital that WWII US General Douglas MacArthur once commended that Taiwan was 'an unsinkable aircraft carrier' of strategic importance. Before the World War II, Taiwan was a colony of Japan after the Qing Empire lost the Jia-Wu Sino-Japanese War in 1895 and signed the Treaty of Shimonoseki. Modern systems of government and public infrastructures were introduced during this period. After the World War II, the Republic of China (R.O.C.) acquired control of Taiwan in line with the Cairo declaration of 1943 and the Potsdam Conference of 1945. From that point of time, especially after the Martial law was declared in 1947, the island was under an authoritarian control by the regime of Chiang Kai-Shek and his political party—Kuomintang (KMT), until late 1980s.

During the period of martial law, the KMT implemented a top-down approach that tightly controlled over the government, including the police, the military, even the civilian arena (e.g., media, education, business associations) (Cao, Huang, & Sun, 2014). Like many other societies of dictatorship in the history, massacre usually is one of the means of extreme control. In modern history of Taiwan, the 228 Incident/Massacre in 1947 left a permanent mark, especially among those directly suffered from the loss of family members or properties. KMT used military force to sharply suppress civil unrests in the community in the name of hunting spies of Chinese Communist Party (CCP). Innocent residents could have been arrested and tortured by the authorities, and an estimated 25 thousand civilians died in the incident (Phillips, 2003). Such an incident quickly generated a chilling effect spreading the atmosphere of *White Terror* in which residents self-censored their expressions for several decades. The experience was especially traumatizing to those were directly impacted by the incident, and some may be afraid to even recall details. Thus, it is understandable that non-KMT and some senior residents might have profound distrust of KMT in particular and authorities in general because of what they experienced or witnessed.

While facing choking political freedom, Taiwan's economic development was directly benefited from U.S. diplomatic policy in the Pacific region. With the U.S. financial aid, Taiwan enjoyed a remarkable economic growth after 1950 despite KMT's strictly social control. The international community recognized this fast-growing period as an "economic miracle" that established the foundation of being one of "Four Little Dragons" (along with Hong Kong, Singapore, and South Korea) in East Asia (Vogel, 1993). However, R.O.C. in Taiwan was internationally marginalized because of a formal diplomatic relation between the U.S. and CCP's People

Republic of China (P.R.C.) built in mid-1970s. Taiwan then (forced to) withdrew from the United Nations (UN) and other international organizations.

The successful economic development transformed Taiwan from an agricultural society to an industrial and commercial one. Urbanization has been an ongoing process since Japanese colony, but this process takes a faster pace, especially after mid-1970s. The global market offered further opportunities of economic growth, and international corporations and capitals brought in occupations that required specialized job skills. Accompanied with the structural changes in the society, traditional family-centered values were gradually replaced by values of non-familial institutions, particularly in cities. The urban life styles become similar to other cities' residents in the modern world, while rural counties are more likely to preserve traditional lifestyle and values.

Taiwanese overall were increasingly adaptive to the western values of diversity, legality, and equality. Collectively, the social, economic, and geopolitical environment provided the fertile soil to breed the seed of democracy on the island that inherent diverse cultures. However, the rural counties have continued to face challenges of losing residents; younger generations moved to cities for higher-pay jobs and career opportunities, and more elders and sometimes children were left in rural areas. Also, the shift of population led to less tax revenues for the local governments and income inequality. In conjunction with dropping birth rate in the society, the general population continuously declined in rural Taiwan.

After implementing for 37 years, Martial law was lifted in 1987 authorized by President Chiang Ching-Kuo, followed by democratization and a series of changes in Constitutions in 1990s and 2000s oversaw by President Lee Teng-Hui. The political transformation satisfied the realistic demands of democracy from the grass root and legalized citizens' political involvement via a representative system of government in Taiwan. Citizens were allowed to organize political parties in a newly burgeoning democratic Taiwan or free from not joining the ruling party (KMT) of the time without concerning consequences (Wang, Sun, Wu, Craen, & Hsu, 2020). In addition, it is worth noting that any political transition often accompanies with conflicts to some extent, and confrontations naturally emerged between the authorities and the citizens. Taiwan was not an exception; incidents like Cheng, a pro-democracy activist and publisher who set himself on fire in 1989 in support of "real" freedom of speech, was an extreme example. The first student protest, for another example, in modern history of Taiwan—Wild Lily Movement—was initiated by students from National Taiwan University in 1990 to seek for fundamental and principal changes regarding how democracy should be practiced (e.g., citizens directly elect the president). This large-scale student-led protest took place at Chiang Kai-Shek Memorial in Taipei (now *Liberty Square*) brought real challenges, both symbolic and practical, of the time to the authorities because a similar student-led protest—Tiananmen Square protest—was out of control 1 year before in Beijing, China. Taiwan's successful and largely peaceful transition was labelled as a "political miracle" by some Western scholars, as the process challenged existing political theories (Clark, 2001).

In the process of democratization, the largest opponent party that gathered non-KMT politicians was Democratic Progressive Party (DPP). These two major parties in Taiwan are substantially different in many ways, such as declaration of sovereignty, interpretations of national independence, practices of democracy, and emphasis on political agendas like foreign policy, environmental protection and economic development. Residents identified themselves with political ideologies held by KMT (pan-blue) and other smaller parties (e.g., People First Party, New Party, non-Partisan Solidarity Union) and those identified themselves with ideologies held by DPP (pan-green) and other smaller parties (e.g., Taiwan Solidarity Union, Taiwan Independence Party, Taiwan State-building Party, New Power Party) have different views and perceptions of governmental entities, including the justice system (Sun, Wu, Triplett, & Wang, 2016). Occasionally, a sense of group identity derived from political affiliation or political ideology can cause serious conflicts in basic unit of social groups/institutions like family, especially during election seasons, in this Asian society. By 2020, Taiwan has practiced democracy to a great extent for more than three decades, and citizens are truly free from *White Terror* to elect their legislative representatives and local executives without concerning coercion and persecution. Citizens have the right to directly vote the top leader of the state in the last seven presidential elections and have used ballots to rotate the ruling party of the central government (KMT: year 1996–2000, year 2008–2016 and DPP: year 2000–2008, year 2016–2024). In 2016, Taiwan also elected the first female President Tsai Ing-wen, who was also the first female top leader in Asian countries.

To the general public, the transition from an authoritarian to a democratic society was characterized by several observable changes, such as the press freedom, formation of labour unions, and education. The media was exempt from the government's forceful control, and TV and radio stations were allowed to compete with those funded by the nation or KMT in a free market environment. In the post-martial law period, the free market has brought serious competitions to private-owned news or media groups, and some stations even use local dialects (e.g., Taiwanese, Hakka) to report news in order to attract certain groups of audience. One of the less desirable consequences is to use sensational topics as the marketing strategy. Hong Kong social activist Lai probably is one of the most noticeable example when his giant media group Apple Daily stepped into Taiwan (BBC News, 2020). Negative news on the authorities, including governmental agencies and political figures, can be appealing and attractive to general audience who were just freed from governmental control of public opinion. Schools were allowed to develop or adopt alternative educational materials and textbooks, and universities began to offer courses covering politically sensitive topics, including the thoughts of communism. Parents could find alternative education for their kids with special needs, such as current Digital Minister Audrey Tang (Leonard, 2020).

Democratization continues to root on the island in the twenty-first century; Taiwanese learn to express political opinions through different avenues while the authorities constrain their power within the boundaries of law. Perhaps inspired by overseas "occupy Wall Street" movement, Sunflower Movement of 2014, which was largely led by college students and greatly supported by different groups of citizens, occupied the congress building (so called *Legislative Yuan*) for more than 3 weeks. The protest aimed to overcome the illegitimate passing of Cross-Strait Service Trade Agreement, which was strongly supported by the Executive branch led by President Ma Ying-Jeou who politically leaned towards China. To some extent, this movement marks citizens' challenges of the dysfunctional elected legislators, governmental malpractice, and directly appealed citizen's constitutional rights. With these social, economic and historical backgrounds of Taiwan, the following section introduces the police system of modern Taiwan.

3.1.1 Modern Police in Taiwan

The role of policing in Taiwan has changed significantly over the past three to four decades, largely because of a major change in political systems upon the lift of Martial Law. Between World War II and the termination of Martial Law in 1987, the police in Taiwan were basically an extended arm of the military to maintain social order. In the historical context of anti-Communism and the social context of police state (so called *White Terror*), law enforcement agencies wielded greater discretion in encounters with citizens. Warrantless searches and arrests were usually used as a mean to suppress different political opinions, and public attitude towards the police can be hostile. As Taiwan has moved toward a democratic political identity in the post-martial law period, authoritarian-oriented approaches were curtailed and police discretion has been regulated by legislation (Cao, Huang, & Sun, 2016) and monitored by citizens. The paradigm change marked a shift in policing functions from preserving the distribution of existing governmental power to serving the public, promoting human rights and press freedoms, taking public opinions into consideration, and proactively preventing crime (Hsieh & Boateng, 2015; Martin, 2013).

Today, there are two major law enforcement agencies in contemporary Taiwan—the National Police Agency (NPA) and the Investigation Bureau (MJIB). Both NPA and MJIB are classified at the same level in the governmental bureaucracy of the executive branch but answer to different centres of authority—the NPA is under the Ministry of Interior, while MJIB is under the Ministry of Justice. Both agencies have the jurisdiction over the entire state, but they are tasked to different priorities of law enforcement.

In terms of function, the NPA is in charge of local law enforcement forces that interact with the general population on a daily basis, and the agency exercises administrative jurisdiction over all police departments and evaluates the performance of police chiefs. NPA officers wear identical uniforms, respond to citizen complaints and emergency requests, patrol streets and issue citations, maintain orders of crowds, and investigate crimes. Members of the agency are stationed in neighborhood-based branches (called *pai-chu-suo*) and engage in community-oriented policing (Sun & Chu, 2006). In the process of democratization, elected local political leaders are legally authorized to appoint their police chiefs from a list of candidates recommended by the NPA (Cao et al., 2014). On the one hand, this governmental structure forces police to respond to local priorities and listen to residents' needs and priorities. In Western democratic societies, political and budgetary constraints can serve to minimize the opportunity that local police misuse power. On the other hand, the contemporary political system in Taiwan predisposes local police leadership on a position that is more sensitive to local political influences.

The function of MJIB is set to emphasize the protection of national security, and thus MJIB agents are tasked to higher degrees of complex missions like counter-terrorism, international anti-money laundry task forces, infiltration prevention, domestic security investigation, and intelligence collection. The MJIB is the Taiwanese official liaison in the Egmont Group Financial Intelligence Units (FIU), and the bureau is functionally equivalent to the U.S. federal law enforcement agencies like the FBI. The director-general of MJIB could be summoned by the president of Taiwan for consultation on high-end intelligence relevant to homeland security. Additionally, the MJIB maintains missions in several embassies, consulates, or Taipei Economic and Cultural Offices to coordinate investigations with international allies. Given the fact that Taiwan does not have many formal diplomatic relations because of China's suppression, the MJIB agents are also tasked to work with allies in a complex environment of foreign affairs.

Both MJIB agents and NPA officers are evaluated by mechanisms of performance appraisal similar to other law enforcement agencies in Taiwan. An incentive, merit-based pay structure is tight to performance evaluation. How officers satisfy internally measured performance criteria depends upon the types of crime-fighting objectives that are the current focus of law enforcement (e.g., clearance rates, DUI enforcement, calls for service), prioritized objectives needing urgent attention (e.g., bombing threats), or special case investigations. Dynamic organizational focus and priorities subsequently defines the corresponding evaluation of performance criteria, which have impacts on officers' rewards, bonuses, and promotions. According to Cao and his colleagues (2014), the police culture of "performance first" in Taiwan substantially impacts workplace morale and may shape decision making. This police culture conditions police officers moving toward meeting organizational goals and occasionally through illegitimate means.

In this emerged democratic society, political allegiances could be found influencing legal authorities, particularly when political struggles broke out between the DPP and the KMT. For instance, in a highly unusual series of moves, the NPA's top leader was replaced four times within an eight-year period, after the DPP's Chen Shui-bian, the first president from a non-KMT party, was elected to run the central government for two terms (from 2000 to 2008). In another example, the Director General of the MJIB, Mr. Yeh was found to be leaking information about certain ongoing investigations to then-President Chen. Mr. Yeh was later convicted for leaking case information about investigations in progress, including money laundry that involved the president. Chen ended his second presidential term amid allegations of corruption, and he was sentenced to prison. Unusual personnel changes in law enforcement and the perception of political patronage led many law enforcement officers to believe that personal connections with politicians were more important than field performance and professional qualifications in deciding promotions.

Through legislative efforts and the passing of the *Civil Service Administrative Neutrality Law* in 2009, the agencies were formally able to institutionalize the separation of political influence from policing (Cao et al., 2014).

In addition to instability in leadership, police in Taiwan continue to face challenges in everyday policing that coincided with rapid changes in the social, economic, and political environment. For instance, urbanization has had a conditioning effect on a wide range of policing strategies, as well as on the public's attitude toward the police in Taiwan (Wang & Sun, 2020). Research also indicates that rural officers are more likely to favor citizen cooperation and consistently demonstrate higher levels of group cohesion and solidarity in comparison to their urban counterparts (Sun & Chu, 2009). As a small island state on a "bare rock" (Friedman, 2005), limited natural resources in Taiwan constantly encourage efficiency in human systems in order to sustain the human society on it. The historical and political context also created long-existing barriers between local and national law enforcement on transparency in intelligence sharing and horizontal lines-of-communication within bureaucratic organizations. Although Taiwan has an overall lower crime rate than most Western countries like U.S. (Chu, 2013), to combat emerged crimes that garner the most public attention and cause the most harm to society such as drugs (Yang, Tzeng, Tai, & Ku, 2020), youth (Steffensmeier, Zhong, & Lu, 2017), high-tech transitional crime (Hsieh & Wang, 2018) and money laundering (Ministry of Justice Investigation Bureau, 2018), cross-agency collaboration is necessary.

3.2 The First Commercial Bank (FCB) ATM Hacking in Taiwan

The outbreak of the First Commercial Bank (FCB) ATM heist in Taiwan is an example of an elaborate virtual hacking intrusion (Sancho, Huq, & Michenzi, 2017), which had not been examined from an academic criminological perspective until Hsieh and Wang (2018)'s study. Initially, the FCB could have been just another case among other at least a hundred other unsolved ATM hacking incidents. However, we now know that the FCB case is a unique way to understand recent and innovated ATM hacking for several reasons.

First, the heist was committed by notorious Eastern European criminals—Carbanak/Cobalt group—who are responsible for a series of financial institution infiltrations in 40 nations. Before committing the FCB offense, the criminal group has profited from more than 100 financial institutions worldwide since 2013 (Reuters, 2018; Taipei Times, 2018). Second, the technique of "jackpotting" has been successfully replicated globally as well as having been employed in the FCB case. Third, it is the first time that foreign organized crime appeared in Taiwan through an ATM heist scheme which has attracted much attention among public, media, and private cyber security companies. Despite conventional *turf jealousies* (Geller & Morris, 1992) that remain within police culture, the collaborative relationship that emerged between local law enforcement (i.e. Notational Police Agency [NPA]) and national policing force (i.e. Ministry of Justice Investigation Bureau [MJIB]) was the linchpin to solving the FCB case as it mobilized community policing and digital and computer forensics together (Wang, Hsieh, Chang, Jiang, & Dallier, 2020). Fourth, Taiwanese authorities efficiently recovered more than 90% of the cash (approximately is 2.4 million US dollars) within a few days. Taiwan is also the first state to arrest, prosecute, convict, and sanction the alleged members of Carbanak/Cobalt group (Devereux, Wild, & Robinson, 2018; Finkle & Wu, 2017). Fifth, the groundwork and the leadership that developed around the FCB case further encouraged Europol, National Crime Agency of Britain, the FBI, Taiwanese authorities along with other states' law enforcement agencies to advance a complex investigation and cross-border cooperation on Cobalt malware attacks. Eventually, the alleged leader of the criminal group was arrested by the Spanish National Police almost 2 years after the crime (Europol, 2018).

Therefore, this unique case demonstrates the nature of the crime of jackpotted ATM hackings and the pioneering efforts of law enforcement investigation in this area. A case study approach is employed here to reconstruct events making up the FCB heist and to examine qualitative data obtained from agency records, including the MJIB investigation report, forensic and analytic reports, police reports, and legal documents. Supplemental information about the media and citizen's responses and social artifacts are also included. To provide additional details and their meaningful interpretation, interactive interviews with NPA police officers and MJIB special agents were also obtained and analyzed.

In total, interview data from two MJIB agents, eight NPA officers, one Immigration Agency officer, and three civilians are analyzed in the present study. The semi-structured interviews were conducted in Mandarin from 2017 to 2018 in Taiwan. A purposive sampling strategy was utilized to identify eligible and potential participants (e.g. criminal justice agents, citizens, media) who had been involved in or connected to components of the FCB case such as case development and management, digital/computer forensics, criminal apprehension, international allies, and public opinion. To meet the standards of confidentiality, we generated code names when referring to their statements. Interview scripts were systematically coded and manually analyzed to retrieve the themes relevant to case clearance, cybersecurity, law enforcement collaborations, and cross-agency competition. Although case study approach in general does not offer generalization, the FCB case shed unique light on this type of modus operandi actually had been replicated by the same group of criminals in many prior cases. Thus, the significance of FCB as a case of cybercrime also offers theoretical implications. The following sections introduce the details of FCB case and present the process of orchestrating an ATM heist.

3.2.1 Computer Forensics and the FCB ATM Hacking

The Carbanak/Cobalt group, made up of European cybercriminals had already successfully completed a number of digital bank robberies across countries using the "Cobalt Strike" penetration that allowed them to further develop a more sophisticated attack using tailor-made malware to penetrate financial institutions (Europol, 2018). In early July 2016, a total of 22 conspirators (of 8 different nationalities) came to Taiwan prepared for an ATM heist (see Table 3.1). Fifteen of them were mules who picked up the cash ejected non-stop (until the money ran out) from targeted ATMs that were already infected and maliciously programmed as jackpotted slot machines. The other seven criminals were tasked to coordinate cash transportation and money laundering (Taiwan High Court, 2017).

From midnight of July 10 to the morning of July 11, the Carbanak/Cobalt group simultaneously launched "jackpotted" hacking attacks on 41 ATMs at 22 branches

Table 3.1 FCB ATM hacking syndicate

Names	Main roles	Arrive date	Departure date
Berezovskiy, Sergey	Team 1: Mules (9 ATMs)	July 6, 2016–July 9, 2016	July 10, 2016–July 13, 2016
Berkman, Vladimir			
Manukian, Gaik	Team 2: Mules (9 ATMs)		
Kamo, Adiian			
Malic, Oleg	Team 3: Mules (8 ATMs)		
Secrieru, Ion			
Velicoglo, Igor			
Babii, Evgenii	Team 4: Mules (5 ATMs)		
Ursu, Vitalie			
Arsenii, Alexandru			
Tann, Xander	Team 5: Mules (6 ATMs)		
Kharechko, Victor			
Gartsman, Yakov	Team 6: Mules (4 ATMs)		
Isurins, Josifs			
Iakubov, Rafik			
Lvovskiy, Alexander	Handling stolen money	July 9, 2016–July 16, 2016	July 11, 2016–July 13, 2016
Sarkisova, Oxana			
Boue, Etienne Pierre Paul			
Peregudovs, Andrejs			N/A (Arrested by NPA in Taiwan)
Colibaba, Mihail			
Pencov, Nicolae			
Freijs, Renars	Communication support (e.g. burner phones, SIM cards)	July 13, 2016	July 18, 2016

Source: Taiwan High Court (2017)

across 3 cities (Taipei, New Taipei, Taichung) just as an intense tropical cyclone/typhoon passed by Taiwan. (Taiwan High Court, 2017) (see Fig. 3.1). On July 11, the FCB filed an official report to the Taiwan Financial Supervisory Commission (FSC) that more than NT $83.3 million dollars (approximately $2.6 million US dollars) was stolen. Whether or not the FCB was specifically selected for hacking or there was some other motivation behind the targeting remains unknown. Yet, one undisputed fact is that a specific ATM model (PC 1500XE) manufactured by the German company Wincor Nixdorf International that has been globally used by financial institutions was singled out for these attacks (Taipei District Prosecutors Office, 2017). On the day of the report, the FCB also suspended withdrawals from 1000 ATMs of the same model.

According to the MJIB cybercrime section Chief, Mr. Chou, the Carbanak/Cobalt group plots hacking in sophisticated ways. The complex modus operandi[1] could be broken down into four stages (see Fig. 3.2). First, digital forensics indicates that unknown hackers penetrated the FCB's branch in London, UK, and accessed the banks' voice recording system from an IP address in Switzerland on May 31, 2016. In this preparation phase, hackers also successfully stole an administrator's credentials using a social engineering approach in order to enter the FCB's Intranet.

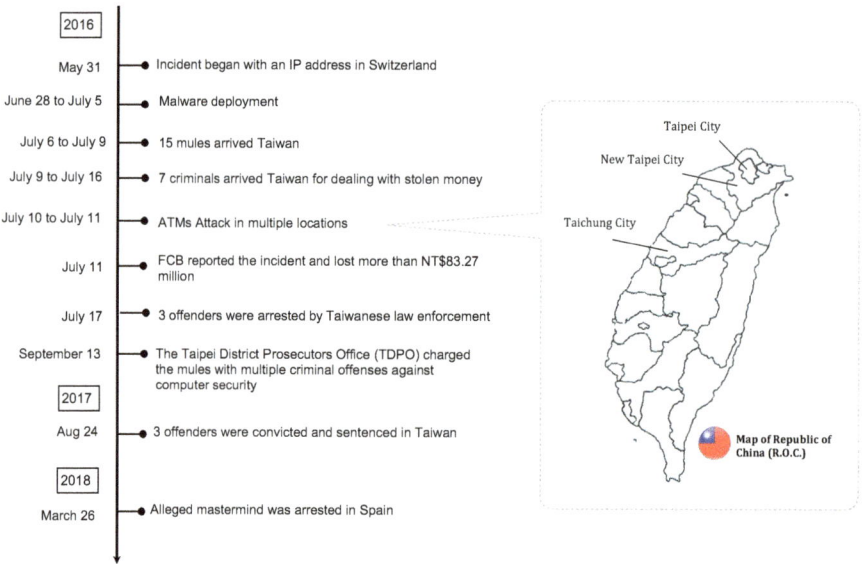

Fig. 3.1 Timeline in brief: FCB ATM heist. Source: Legal documents (e.g., Taipei District Prosecutors Office, High Court, Supreme court), Press release (e.g., Europol, MJIB)

---

[1] https://www.youtube.com/watch?v=KpnY2-WjybA

3.2 The First Commercial Bank (FCB) ATM Hacking in Taiwan

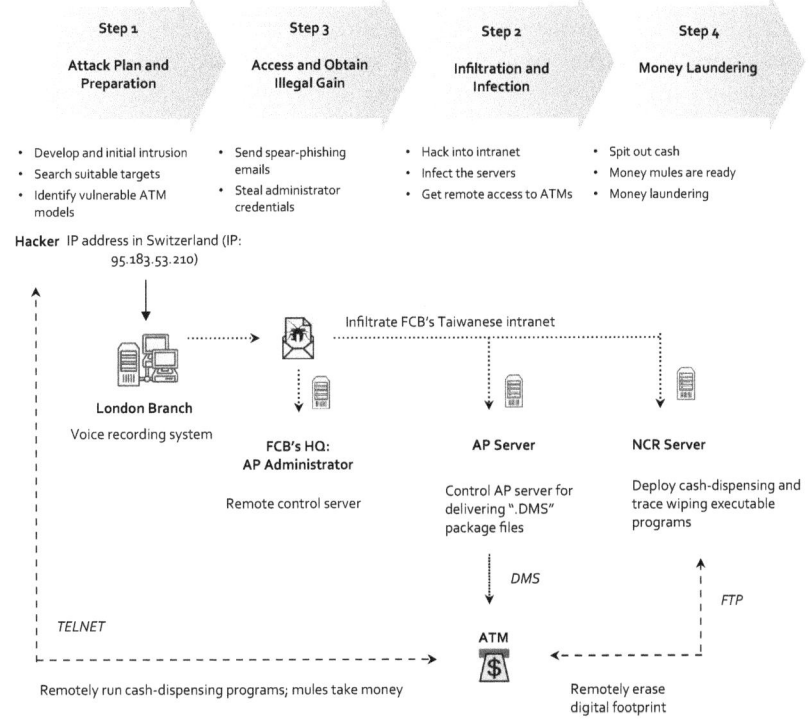

Fig. 3.2 FCB network attack. Sources: Hsieh and Wang (2018); Wang, Hsieh, et al. (2020)

Second, given that the FCB's voice recording system had been compromised, hackers could infect internal FCB's servers. For instance, there were five executable files related to cash-dispensing (i.e., cnginfo.exe, cngdisp.exe, cngdisp_new.exe) and trace-wiping (i.e., cleanup.bat, sdelete.exe) that were smoothly dispatched on the National Cash Register (NCR) server. The cash dispensing files, in this case, were used to control infected ATMs to allow the process of dispensing an uninterrupted stream of cash. Trace-wiping files such as the ones used here allowed the hackers to completely delete the digital evidence of having invaded the ATMs' hard drive. Moreover, hackers then breached other employees' computers in Taiwan's FCB's headquarters which paved the way for gaining remote control over the application server (AP) frameworks. AP servers usually store and disseminate software update packages to ATMs.

Third, once the AP servers were taken over, hackers were able to deliver unauthorized commands from the bank's processing center to the AP servers. In other words, they uploaded and delivered fake "update" package files (with the file extension ".DMS") that are only recognized by ATMs. After loading the fake "update" package files into the ATMs, the ATMs computer would turn on a telnet service that enables a connection between the hackers' remote computers and the computers within the infected ATMs. Meanwhile, the fake "update" package would build a file transfer protocol (FTP) connection which allow ATM computers to download pre-installed executable files from the NCR server (mentioned above in the second step). It took the hackers less than 2 weeks to complete the malware deployment (see Fig. 3.1) on the targeted ATMs. The entire pre-cyberattack preparation was swift—from the voice recording system breached in London, to Intranet infiltration, to ATM malware infection—it took about 6 weeks (Group-IB & Fox-IT, n.d.).

Finally, 15 mules were divided into 6 teams and spread out in three cities (Taiwan High Court, 2017). Beginning at midnight, July 10 until the next morning, once the mules were in position they started to contact the hackers, and then the hackers remotely controlled the targeted ATMs via telnet service and executed pre-dispatched programs for cash dispensing. The digital forensics further indicate that on July 12, hackers executed the trace-wiping files to wipe out any digital footprint (discussed above in phase two and phase three) along with the file (i.e., displog.txt) that resulted from the clearance execution. The telecommunication means between money mules and behind-scene criminals was professionally prepared. As an investigator indicated:

> These criminals are very professional (wiping out trace) in the telecommunication (on phones and software). (Chief "C2", Third Precinct, Keelung City Police Bureau)

Because it was the criminal syndicate's intent to completely destroy all digital evidence of penetration into the ATMs, it was feared that it would be difficult to reconstruct the modus operandi and to ascertain how the ATMs were sabotaged by the hackers. However, it appeared that all that would be needed was for the hackers to make one mistake, as investigators relate,

> …after investigating 40 more ATMs [targeted by the criminals], we found a Trojan horse computer malware on a bank branch's ATM, not the rest of branches. Hackers might omit or forget to wipe out the evidence… (Supervisor "C4", CID)

> …when we processed computer forensics on [FCB's] 41 ATMs, every ATM was clean except for one ATM where hackers did not completely cover their mark. We found a partial digital footprint left, and this is enough to prompt us to trace them [hackers] back…It feels like, "Jackpot!" to us and we were confident that we could reconstruct his [hacker's] MO…. but to be honest, if the hacker(s) did not make a mistake and had everything [digital evidence] destroyed completely, we might not be able to understand the whole picture of the ATM heist efficiently and completely. It would definitely take a great deal of extra time and effort to get inside of their game and figure out exactly how they take over ATMs and what programming they carry out…maybe, even after all of our efforts had been tried, this would still hit a dead end. And FCB would be just like one of many financial institutions that suffered a great lost (Special Agent "S", MJIB)

It was explained that "about 4 percent of Taiwan's national ATM network of 27,200 machines are affected" (Reuters, 2016). However, it is unclear whether all of these infected ATMs were caused by the FCB cyberattack or if different hackers or organized crime penetrated them at different time points. This question requires further investigation.

3.2.2 Mules and Men for Money Laundering

Admittedly, the FCB incident was well orchestrated and coordinated by the Carbanak/Cobalt group. In addition to the hackers working remotely, mules (15) and other offenders (7) played specific roles in order to complete an array of different tasks to complete the heist. The role of mules is relatively straightforward compared to the rest of the offenders. They arrived in Taiwan between July 6th and July 9th, collected cash from ATMs on the day of ATM attacks, bagged the cash and delivered the stolen money to other offenders or designated locations where their accomplices were waiting. Soon after the tasks were done, the mules all departed over the period of July 10th to July 13th (Taiwan High Court, 2017). None of the mules were apprehended in Taiwan.

The remaining seven offenders arrived in Taiwan between July 9th and July 16th. Each of them coordinated with different mules to retrieve the stolen cash and then transport, transfer and hide the cash securely before their departure, despite the fact that they might not know or meet with each other in advance. To avoid detection by law enforcement, these criminals changed lodgings from time to time and used burner phones with disposable numbers and SIM cards. The criminals packaged cash with backpacks, duffel bags, carry-on luggage, spinner suitcases and even with trash bags to avoid attention. They carefully transferred these "packages" to different locations to hide or to store temporarily including hotel rooms, rented apartments/Airbnbs, a mountain park nearby Taipei, and in public lockers (see Fig. 3.3) at the convergence of the Taipei Railroad Station and the Taipei mass rapid transit (MRT) station (Taiwan High Court, 2017). Four out of the seven offenders allegedly carried some of these packages as they left Taiwan between July 11th and July 18th.

Perhaps without zealous citizens providing tips to the police, Taiwanese authority may not have even noticed that there was an ongoing cyberattack (Taipei District Prosecutors Office, 2017). About 20 h after the heist on July 10th, two citizens reported suspicious behavior that occurred at the GuTing Branch of the FCB to the NPA. As civilian comments:

> I think that citizens voluntarily reported to the police when noticed unusual ATM activities is essential to the FCB case. (Journalist, "L2")

According to their description, one of two foreigners nervously rushed out from an ATM machine when the cash was still in the cash dispenser while the other person waited in the taxi (Taipei District Prosecutors Office, 2017). These two foreigners were later identified as two of the mules, Gaik Manukian and Adiian Kamo. At this point, the NPA and the FCB had no clue about the ATM hacking scheme yet. The next morning around 2 A.M. (July 11th), another two mules (Sergey Berezovskiv and Vladiair Berkman) were withdrawing cash from an ATM at the Nanmen Branch of the FCB. A passerby boldly confronted their suspicious behavior with physical contact. In the process, Berezovskiv unknowingly dropped his credit card as they fled the scene. Later the same day, the FCB reported the loss of millions of New Taiwan dollars from ATMs which immediately made headlines and breaking news

Fig. 3.3 Taipei Railroad Station public lockers

all over the media. However, the information concerning Berezovskiv's credit card gave the police a good place to start looking into the incident along with the identity of this probable accessory. The NPA mobilized resources, "reviewed over 1500 street monitors [CCTV], 212 immigration reports, 500 hotels, 28 websites and Facebook accounts of suspects, and logs from 23 taxis and 15 buses used by the suspects" (Taipei District Prosecutors Office, 2017 p. 255) and soon a picture began to form of 22 criminals who were linked to the FCB heist. On July 17th, three offenders (Andrejs Peregudovs, Mihail Colibaba, Nicolae Pencov) were arrested by the NPA (see Liberty Times, 2018).

3.2.3 Aftermath

A total of NT$ 77.48 million in cash (approximately 2.4 million US dollars) was recovered by Taiwanese authorities which accounts for approximately 90% of all the stolen cash. By the middle of September, 2016, the Taipei District Prosecutors Office had charged three offenders with multiple crimes carrying a possible 12-year sentence for each (Taipei District Prosecutors Office, 2017). The court sanctioned 4 years 10 months, 4 years 8 months, and 4 years 6 months for Peregudovs, Colibab, and Pencov respectively (Supreme Court, 2017; Taiwan High Court, 2017).

It may be argued that Taiwanese authorities "got lucky" in the clearance of the FCB's case because the hackers accidentally left digital evidence in one of the targeted ATMs and underestimated the capacity of computer forensics and the competence of law enforcement. A MJIB agent responds,

> Being a criminal justice official in Taiwan, we all know Dr. Henry Lee, a famous forensic scientist. He helped with many high-profile cases such as O. J. Simpson, and the re-investigation of John F. Kennedy among others. He shared the "theory of table legs" in crime investigation many times in his speeches. Of course, the intactness of crime scenes, physical evidence, and witnesses [three legs] are important to present but don't forget, another [leg] is "luck". So, yes, we need luck in this case. But don't get me wrong, I didn't say we couldn't solve the case without luck….again, I didn't say we are the best, but we do have sophisticated digital and commuter forensic skills and a great capacity to reconstruct incidents. These are credits, and should not be buried. Otherwise, I don't think that the FBI would want to work with us on some cases… (Special Agent "S", MJIB)

The Carbanak/Cobalt group has been identified as responsible for the cumulative losses of over one billion Euros globally as well as the highest gain per heist at up to ten million Euros (Europol, 2018). Taiwanese authorities' investigation experiences on the FCB ATM hacking case provided significant intelligence to other countries that were victims of the same group, allowing them to explore and expand their investigations on cyberattacks. On March 26, 2018, the leader of the cyberattack syndicate behind the Carbanak/Cobalt group (Denis K.) was arrested in Alicante, Spain, in a joint law enforcement operation (e.g. Europol, Taiwan, Belarus, Romania, Spain, Moldova, United States) (Europol, 2018; Reuters, 2018).

According to Spain's Interior Ministry, during the raid in Alicante, the police seized luxury cars and jewels worth 500,000 Euros and frozen bank accounts and two homes valued at about one million Euros. Denis K. had directed the criminal organization since 2013 and he converted the stolen cash into cryptocurrency. To further laundering money, he also set up an "enormous network" to mine Bitcoins. At the time of his arrest, he held accumulated about 15,000 Bitcoins (Reuters, 2018).

Denis K. worked with three other gang members without personal contact and conducted spear-phishing attacks on bank employees in the preparation phase of cyberattack. Criminals did not know each other but communicating via chat rooms online. They also worked with mafias to facilitate low-level job on ATM heist (Devereux, 2018; Schwartz, 2018). As Spanish National Police says,

Despite the high technical level of its members, the cybercriminals needed the support from other criminal groups to coordinate the work of the "mules" in charge of withdrawing cash from ATMs that it attacked in different countries... (Schwartz, 2018)

Russian mafia gangs were responsible for supplying the required mules until 2015 and Moldovan mafia gangs started for this in 2016 (Devereux, 2018; Reuters, 2018; Schwartz, 2018). However, how many 22 criminals identified in FCB's case currently or formerly related to either Russian or Moldovan mafia gangs or connected to other unknown gangs remain unclear. At this point, there is also no further released information about Denis K.'s punishment status. Nevertheless, the Chief Executive Office of the European Banking Federation (EBF) commented the international police cooperation,

It clearly goes beyond raising awareness on cybersecurity and demonstrates the value of our partnership with the cybercrime specialists at Europol. Public-private cooperation is essential when it comes to effectively fighting digital cross-border crimes like the one [ATM heist] that we are seeing here with the Carbanak gang. (Europol, 2018).

Broadly speaking, the FCB case might indeed contribute to this considerable success for a join force police cooperation against a high-profile cybercriminal syndicate with a high technical level of modus operandi. Steven Wilson, Head of Europol's European Cybercrime Centre (EC3) also concluded,

This global operation is a significant success for international police cooperation against a top level cybercriminal organization. The arrest of the key figure in this crime group illustrates that cybercriminals can no longer hide behind perceived international anonymity. This is another example where the close cooperation between law enforcement agencies on a worldwide scale and trusted private sector partners is having a major impact on top level cybercriminality. (Europol, 2018)

3.3 Cases After FCB

Only 1 month after FCB case, the criminal group used ATM hacking and robbed approximate US $346 k cash from 21 ATMs of Government Savings Bank in Thailand. Although the Taiwanese authority successfully arrested three criminals, identify the rest of suspects, and recovered the vast majority of cash "robbed" from ATMs in FCB case, there was no formal or diplomatic avenues to collaborate with the international community.

A series of ATM hackings also occurred in north American, including U.S. and Mexico, in 2017 (Rudnitsky, 2017). The cyber attackers used a specific malware to infect targeted ATMs' hard drive in order to dispense cash. In January 2018, such type of attacks continued to invade the United States, and the US Secret Service and major ATM providers NCR and Diebold Nixdorf issued warnings about the threat of ATM hacking. The criminals emptied targeted ATM dispensers with malware and hacking remotely.

The development of similar cases done by Carbanak/Cobalt group indicates that the transnational criminal group has a very clear target of ATMs. In addition, the criminal groups were not deterred by the law enforcement across countries, although three members were caught by Taiwanese law enforcement. In order to successfully "rob" ATMs globally, the criminal group appears to carefully plan many details, including spear phishing, hacking, cyberattacks, telecommunication, and evidence-erasing.

References

BBC News. (2020, August 12). Jimmy Lai: Arrested Hong Kong tycoon tells protesters to be 'careful.' Retrieved October 10, 2020, from https://www.bbc.com/news/world-asia-china-53748285
Cao, L., Huang, L., & Sun, I. (2014). *Policing in Taiwan: From authoritarianism to democracy*. London, UK: Routledge.
Cao, L., Huang, L., & Sun, I. (2016). From authoritarian policing to democratic policing: A case study of Taiwan. *Policing & Society, 26*(6), 642–658.
Chu, D. C. (2013). Crime and criminal justice issues in Taiwan. *International Journal of Comparative and Applied Criminal Justice, 37*(2), 75–78.
Clark, C. (2001). Successful democratization in the ROC: Creating a security challenge. In A. C. Tan, S. Chan, & C. Jillson (Eds.), *Taiwan's national security: Dilemmas and opportunities* (pp. 18–59). Aldershot: Ashgate.
Devereux, C. (2018, March 27). Mastermind behind ATM malware attacks arrested in Spain. *Insurance Journal*. Retrieved October 13, 2020, from https://www.insurancejournal.com/news/international/2018/03/27/484454.htm
Devereux, C., Wild, F. & Robinson, E. (2018, June 25). The biggest digital heist in history isn't over yet. Retrieved October 10, 2020 from https://www.bloomberg.com/news/features/2018-06-25/the-biggest-digital-heist-in-history-isn-t-over-yet
Europol. (2018, March 26). *Mastermind behind Euro 1 billion cyber bank robbery arrested in Spain*. Retrieved October 13, 2020, from http://www.europol.europa.eu/newsroom/news/mastermind-behind-eur-1-billion-cyber-bank-robbery-arrested-in-spain
Finkle, J., & Wu, J. R. (2017, January 4). Taiwan ATM heist linked to European hacking spree: Security firm. *Reuters*. Retrieved October 10, 2020, from https://www.reuters.com/article/us-taiwan-cyber-atms/taiwan-atm-heist-linked-to-european-hacking-spree-security-firm-idUSKBN14P0CX
Friedman, T. L. (2005). *The world is flat: A brief history of the twenty-first century*. New York, NY: Farrar, Straus and Giroux.
Geller, W. A., & Morris, N. (1992). Relations between federal and local police. In M. Tonry & N. Morris (Eds.), *Modern policing* (pp. 231–348). Chicago, IL: University of Chicago Press.
Group-IB & Fox-IT. (n.d.). Anunak: APT Against Financial Institutions.
Hsieh, M.-L., & Boateng, F. (2015). Perceptions of democracy and trust in the criminal justice system: A comparison between mainland China and Taiwan. *International Criminal Justice Review, 25*(2), 153–173.
Hsieh, M.-L., & Wang, S.-Y. K. (2018). Routine activities in a virtual space: A Taiwanese case of an ATM hacking spree. *International Journal of Cyber Criminology, 12*(1), 333–352.
Leonard, A. (2020, July 23). How Taiwan's unlikely digital minister hacked the pandemic: Audrey tang says tech can build trust, tame misinformation, and strengthen democracy. Her plan might even work in the US. Retrieved from https://www.wired.com/story/how-taiwans-unlikely-digital-minister-hacked-the-pandemic/
Liberty Times. (2018, March 26). Retrieved October 10, 2020, from https://news.ltn.com.tw/news/society/breakingnews/2377268

Martin, J. T. (2013). Police as linking principle: Rethinking police culture in contemporary Taiwan. In W. Garriott (Ed.), *Policing and contemporary governance*. New York: Palgrave Macmillan. https://doi.org/10.1057/9781137309679_7.

Ministry of Justice Investigation Bureau. (2018). *Anti-money laundering annual report, 2017*. Taiwan: Ministry of Justice Investigation Bureau.

Phillips, S. E. (2003). *Between assimilation and Independence: The Taiwanese encounter nationalist China, 1945–1950*. Stanford, CA: Stanford University Press.

Reuters. (2016, July 17). Taiwan says foreign suspects arrested over $2 million ATM cyber robbery. Retrieved October 13, 2020, from https://www.reuters.com/article/us-taiwan-banks-theft/taiwan-says-foreign-suspects-arrested-over-2-million-atm-cyber-robbery-idUSKCN0ZX0N7

Reuters. (2018, March 26). Spanish police arrest suspected mastermind of $1 billion bank hacks. Retrieved October 13, 2020, from https://www.reuters.com/article/us-cyber-banks-spain/spanish-police-arrest-suspected-mastermind-of-1-billion-bank-hacks-idUSKBN1H21H3

Rudnitsky, J. (2017, December 12). Russian-speaking Hackers Steal $10 M from U.S., Russia Banks: Cyber Security Firm. Retrieved October 10, 2020, from https://www.insurancejournal.com/news/international/2017/12/12/473791.htm

Sancho, D., Huq, N., & Michenzi, M. (2017). *Cashing in on ATM malware: A comprehensive look at various attack types*. Retrieved October 10, 2020, from https://documents.trendmicro.com/assets/white_papers/wp-cashing-in-on-atm-malware.pdf

Schwartz, M. J. (2018, March 27). Spain busts alleged kingpin behind prolific malware. *Bank Info Security*. Retrieved October 13, 2020, from https://www.bankinfosecurity.com/spain-busts-alleged-kingpin-behind-prolific-malware-a-10745

Steffensmeier, D., Zhong, H., & Lu, Y. (2017). Age and its relation to crime in Taiwan and the United States: Invariant, or does cultural context matter? *Criminology, 55*(2), 377–404.

Sun, I., Wu, Y., Triplett, R., & Wang, S.-Y. K. (2016). Media, political party orientation, and public perceptions of police in Taiwan. *Policing: An International Journal of Police Strategies and Management, 39*(4), 694–709.

Sun, I. Y., & Chu, D. (2006). Attitudinal differences between Taiwanese and American police officers. *Policing: An International Journal of Police Strategies & Management, 29*, 190–210.

Sun, I. Y., & Chu, D. C. (2009). Rural v. urban policing: A study of Taiwanese officers' occupational attitudes. *The Police Journal, 82*, 222–246.

Supreme Court. (2017). *Zì gāo fǎ yuàn 106 nián tái shàng zì dì 2603 hào xíng shì pàn jué*. Taipei, Taiwan: Supreme Court.

Taipei District Prosecutors Office. (2017). *Top 10 financial fraud investment records*. Taipei, Taiwan: Taipei District Prosecutors Office.

Taipei Times. (2018, March 28). Suspected leader in 2016 ATM heist arrested in Spain. Retrieved October 10, 2020, from http://taipeitimes.com/News/taiwan/archives/2018/03/28/2003690202

Taiwan High Court. (2017). *Tái wān gāo děng fǎ yuan 106 nián shàng sù zì dì 593 hào xíng shì pàn jué*. Taipei, Taiwan: Taiwan High Court.

Vogel, E. F. (1993). *The four little dragons: The spread of industrialization in East Asia*. Cambridge, MA: Harvard University Press.

Wang, S.-Y. K., Hsieh, M.-L., Chang, C., Jiang, P.-S., & Dallier, D. (2020). Collaboration between law enforcement agencies in combating cybercrime. *International Journal of Offender Therapy and Comparative Criminology*. https://doi.org/10.1177/0306624X20952391.

Wang, S.-Y. K., Sun, I., Wu, Y., Van Craen, W., & Hsu, K. K.-L. (2020). Does trusting in supervisors translate to compliance and cooperation? A test of internal procedural justice among Taiwanese police officers. *Australian and New Zealand Journal of Criminology, 53*(3): 433–453.

Wang, S.-Y. K., & Sun, I. Y. (2020). A comparative study of rural and urban residents' trust in police in Taiwan. *International Criminal Justice Review, 30*(2), 197–218. https://doi.org/10.1177/1057567718763724.

Yang, S.-L., Tzeng, S., Tai, S.-F., & Ku, Y.-C. (2020). Illegal drug use among adolescents in schools and facilities: 3-year surveys in Taiwan. *Asian Journal of Criminology, 15*, 45–63. https://doi.org/10.1007/s11417-019-09292-1.

Chapter 4
Implications of FCB Case

Abstract The FCB case is an unique ATM hacking incident that was successfully solved by Taiwanese law enforcement, while hundreds of similar cases occurred internationally and unsolved. These ATM hackings share very similar modus operandi, and thus the FCB case offers many generalizable implications in practice and theory. This chapter concludes with discussing development of similar cybercrime likely to occur in the COVID-19 and post-pandemic time.

Keywords Policing · Collaboration · Turf jealousy · Routine activity theory · Social engineering · Phishing · Cyber security · COVID-19 pandemic

This chapter covers an array of implications derived from the analysis of FCB case. In the social context of the study site—Taiwan, the following sections discuss the case from several aspects, including inter law enforcement agencies collaboration, media, police-citizen cooperation, and international collaboration. We offer suggestions of cybersecurity to similar organizations, policy recommendations of co-production of cyber security, and contributions to the development of cyber criminology.

4.1 Implication in Policing

Combating borderless cybercrime often requires collaborations across jurisdictions, and sometimes even across physical boundaries of states and countries. To successfully crack down organized cybercrime and bring criminals to justice, effective investigation requires competent computer and digital forensic skills. Understanding how cybercrimes operate in general and modus operandi of digital robbery in specific are prerequisites. Organizing collaborations among investigating law enforcement agencies with different capacities and strengths seems inevitable (James & Warren, 2010). Furthermore, the FCB case demonstrated positive impacts of community-oriented policing (COP) and a *good relationship between citizens and the police* in local communities. Taiwanese citizens were eager to contact the police and to provide information that subsequently led to the arrest of three bagmen.

> Initially, citizens reported to the police that some foreigners suspiciously withdrew money without touching ATMs. Another citizen reported that a pile of NT $60,000 dollars was left on the floor next to an ATM. I personally think these citizens' reports are important because we [law enforcement] might not even notice the incident even after all suspects left Taiwan. (Detective "T1", CID).

> I was impressed by enthusiasm of three citizens who made [initial] reports to the police…when the news of suspects was broadcasted on mass media, an Airbnb owner who happened to host a suspect contacted us right away (Chief "C2", Third Precinct, Keelung City Police Bureau)

> …one of the suspects reserved a room through Airbnb…we also obtained digital evidence like wifi and resident's information from a host of Airbnb (Deputy Supervisor "H1", CID)

> Taiwanese police often promote citizen-police collaboration [community policing]…in the case of FCB, when we [journalists] put suspects' pictures in press, there were some positive effects [in investigation]—general public began to pay attention on what suspects look like. (Journalist, "L2")

> My personal assessment is that at least eighty percent of citizens would cooperate with the police in crime prevention. (Journalist, "A1")

> Taiwanese citizens are indeed enthusiastic and alerted [about crime]…I think that coordinated collaboration [of law enforcement] in many aspects leads to a good outcome of the case. (Special Agent "L").

Before a collaborative relationship between the NPA and the MJIB was developed in the FCB case, there were issues raised within the police regarding jurisdiction. The analysis of interviews also revealed that collaboration operates at local level experience some estrangement from their counterparts (Cohen, 2017). This may result from *intra-agency "turf jealousies"* of both physical territory and authoritative jurisdictions in general (Geller & Morris, 1992) and "performance-first" Taiwanese police culture in particular (Cao, Huang, & Sun, 2014). Intelligence sharing between local police agencies were somewhat blocked at the inception, despite citizens generally are enthusiastic reporting suspicious activities to the police. Several interviewees recalled:

> There seems to be some awkward structure of coordination at the beginning of FCB investigation from an outsider's viewpoint (Journalist, "L2")

> At the beginning of the FCB case, it was thought [by the NPA police] to be a regular fraud ring where a member was sent to pick up the cash [from an ATM]…It feels like that there was a lack of one central command during the initial stage of investigation. Different police branches provided inconsistent lists of suspects for investigating the same case. While everyone worked on the same case, they were holding different levels of information and resources. We [the police] might have wasted a lot of time on not sharing and integrating intelligence internally. (Detective "T1", CID)

4.1 Implication in Policing

> At the beginning of investigation, it was a bottom-up, not top-down approach that it is supposed to be, which is time consuming...we surveyed each banks for potential victimization of ATM hacking and then narrowed down to First Commercial Bank only... ATM hacking happened all over the different jurisdictions...initially, many police precincts set a special task force [for a part of this FCB case]...we [local police] lost direction on the investigation and were unsure what happened...should we use the NPA to lead the case and ask all precincts to share resources and cooperate with the investigation? (Chief "C2", Third Precinct, Keelung City Police Bureau)

In democratic societies, collaboration across law enforcement agencies has been a controversial part in operation. Competition for budget, resources, and even reputation (so called "turf jealousies") between agencies are well-known disincentives of cooperation (Geller & Morris, 1992). In Taiwan, the NPA is the central agency that evaluates performance of local police chiefs, and any formal task force and collaboration between local police departments is supposed to be under NPA's supervision. Although both NPA and MJIB are organized at the same hierarchical level within the central government, the NPA tends to have a better working relationship with other law enforcement agencies than with the MJIB. Several interviewed NPA officers mentioned their collaborations with the Immigration Agency, the Airport Police, and other agencies responsible for homeland security during the investigation. As several interviewees pointed out:

> ...we closely worked with the Airport Police and Immigration Agency on narrowing down the identities of suspects...the collaboration is seamless...one of the suspects escaped to I-Lan county, and we also worked with the Coast Guard to prevent smuggling. (Commander "L1", Criminal Investigation Division [CID]).

> When we learned that suspects are foreigners, we quickly worked with Immigration Agency, the Airport Police, and International Affairs Bureau [of CID] to clarify their identities and to check whether they have passed customs and border...we also worked with Customs Agency and the Coast Guard. (Supervisor "C1", CID)

> ...we worked with Immigration Agency and the Airport Police to obtain their synchronous records of suspects. (Chief "C2", Third Precinct, Keelung City Police Bureau)

> ...we often work with NPA and MJIB, as well as Prosecutors Offices...our agency's collaborations are all based on law. (Chief "L3", Immigration Agency)

Because the MJIB is missioned to prioritize a number of large-scale crime investigations at the national level, such as counter-terrorism, public corruption, white-collar crime (e.g. economic crime, money laundry) and cybercrime, financial institutions tend to approach MJIB, if they decide to seek for help from the authorities. As NPA officers indicated:

> ...for dealing with financial related crimes, [by law] MJIB has the priority...therefore, FCB approached MJIB to file the financial loss and criminal complaints in the first place. (Supervisor "C1", CID)

> Financial industry is reluctant and unwilling to file incident reports with us [the police], and they tend to report to MJIB...because they believe that MIJB would handle cases well, while the police might leak information for media coverage. (Commander "L1", CID)

Conventionally, financial institutions and corporations might choose to cover up cyber incidents out of concerning non-financial implications, such as damaging reputation/image of the business, losing customer confidence and their confidential information, diminishing productivity, compromising business secret and intellectual property, and possibly damaging the status of working relations with regulating authorities (Taylor, Fritsch, Liederbach, & Holt, 2011). The cost of non-financial damage by cyberattacks is difficult to accurately estimate (Antonescu & Birau, 2015). In this case, however, the FCB decided to work with law enforcement agencies from the inception, and one strategy was to broadcast the news of the ATM hacking and distribute the suspects' photos through all types of media coverage right after the cash was stolen. Because of the mass media coverage after a significant large amount of cash were stolen from FCB's ATMs, citizens were able to identify suspects and report their suspicious behaviors standing in front of ATMs with backpacks, in turn, leading to the arrest of three bagmen.

> When working with the media, we have to first understand the case thoroughly…after understanding the whole picture of the case, we (police) can then direct the content of released news. Also, we can understand what the media is interested in their report before news conference. (Supervisor "C4", CID)

The police culture of "performance first" sometimes might blur the missions of crime fighting across levels of policing. A high-profile criminal case that attracts national attention might increase incremental *competition* and even *inter-agency "turf jealousies"* between law enforcement agencies with overlapping jurisdictions. The FCB ATM hacking case showed some signs of "turf jealousies" in the subculture of the police, as well as urgent demands of inter-agency collaboration. As interviewees commented:

> Let me put it in this way, MJIB investigates two [significant] cases per year, while we police have to handle a case every other day, but people believe MJIB agents are of higher quality than us. If I could just work on two cases per year, I could do better investigations. So, this is an apple-and-orange comparison which cannot be practical. I worked with MJIB before, and I think NPA's investigation capacity is no less than MJIB… MJIB takes the lead in computer forensics [in FCB case]…but MJIB does not have a good working relationship with NPA… They [MJIB] would like to grow their capacity for digital forensics, but I think NPA has compatible abilities in this area…in the current case, we [NPA] worked on investigating malware intrusion that MJIB would like to take over… (Commander "L1", CID)

> …our roles [in FCB case] are liaison of international law enforcement agencies and data analysis, including digital forensics, and this is our strength… but we are competing with MJIB in the area of digital forensic (Supervisor "C4", CID)

> MJIB primarily communicate through Taipei District Prosecutors Office because of its leading role in investigation…we could have more meetings [to facilitate resource sharing] (Special Agent "L")

Working with citizens and taking their priority into considerations would increase public trust of the police and enhance legitimacy of the authorities in democracy (Sunshine & Tyler, 2003; Tyler, 1990). While citizens were eager to cooperate and enthusiastically reported suspicious activities to the police in this time-sensitive

4.1 Implication in Policing 37

FCB case, media management remains an important element in high-profile cases. If the consensus of a working protocol is not built across law enforcement agencies, *public relations with citizens and the media* may be compromised.

> I was surprised by an unanticipated media conference hosted by the authority…Other than cooperating and facilitating law enforcement's criminal investigation, I did not plan to reveal my identity publicly. (Citizen "T2")

> …the investigation of the FCB case received much grass root support from the citizens…we manipulated this case and characterized it as outside perpetrators committing crimes in Taiwan on the mass media. (Commander "L1", CID)

> regarding media management, I think that there needs to be a balance between people's right to know and confidentiality of on-going investigations…of course we do not want to reveal too much details about criminal techniques that (some) citizens may imitate…we view this approach is a method of preventing crime. (Deputy Supervisor "H1", CID)

> To the media, we will never have enough news… (Journalist "A1")

In terms of cybercrime fighting, the FCB case confirmed that there are *strong incentives* for inter law enforcement agencies collaborations when an individual or a group of criminals operates across jurisdictions or state/national borders and caused substantial damages (e.g., international terrorism, Kevin Mitnick, Carbanak/Cobalt group). The *complexity* of the FCB case involving both traditional crime investigation strategies and advanced technologies to combat ATM hacking further highlights the need of collaboration for both local police (NPA) and the national agencies (MJIB, Immigration Agency, Coast Guard). The emerged collaborative relationship between NPA and MJIB is congruent with Mitchell, O'Leary, and Gerard's (2015) observation whereby law enforcement collaboration between agencies would develop because of the need for innovative and creative approaches to break the deadlock, improve operations, and achieve desired outcomes. Cross-agency collaboration allows authorities to take full advantage of the *additional investigative skills and prosecutorial tools* necessary to deal with criminals that exist both in physical and virtual environments. Partnership is an essential toolkit to establish efficient channels for information exchange across agencies (Mitchell et al., 2015). The police officers explained:

> …despite concerns in the current [FCB] case, MJIB are in charge of the computer forensic investigation…and we agree with their [crime investigation] perspectives presented in the indictment. (Commander "C3", CID)

> … I believe this [FCB] case should be considered as two parts. First, someone needs to get the money back because this is a heist case, and later on, we need to establish where the bagmen go and how the money would be laundered. These all rely on our [local police] investigation in the physical environment in local communities… (Supervisor "C4", CID)

> Even though we might have miscommunication and disagreement with MJIB on dealing with this [FCB] case, we still built a good collaborative channel with them…one thing is undeniable, the MJIB has professional expertise in computer forensics and we receive training from them, the NPA needs to learn more in this area. (Supervisor "C1", CID)

In conjunction with several mistakes made by the criminals, a *cohesive collaboration* of national-local law enforcement and *clearly separated and focused tasks* among investigating law enforcement agencies is the key that Taiwanese authorities could solve the FCB case within a week (Wang, Hsieh, Chang, Jiang, & Dallier, 2020). In addition, the front-line coverage of FCB case accompanied with lots of public attention and pressure, which pushed collaboration on roles of *network* and *leadership* among law enforcement agencies (Waugh & Streib, 2006). Subsequently, supplemental supports from each side of local and national agencies can be integrated—the MJIB effectively processed computer forensics, while the NPA broadcasted suspects' information to the general public, tracked and seized the stolen cash, and arrested suspects. The cross-agency collaboration also enabled authorities to allocate large-scale resources in this high-profile case in a timely manner. NPA officers acknowledged that effective leadership is important within the police, especially to frontline responders.

> The positive outcome for this [FCB case] was a result of collaboration across law enforcement agencies and legal authorities…[solving the cybercrime] might not be possible, if not to mobilize large scale resources (Special Agent "L")

> I think that the priority of investigation was to identify and arrest suspects and recover the stolen cash…MJIB was in charge of digital forensics…so, in this sense, we were not really competing with MJIB on digital forensics in FCB case. (Supervisor "C4", CID).

> MJIB presents digital forensic evidence and sort out the modus operandi, and we [NPA] figure out how to get the money back and search and apprehend the bagmen… (Supervisor "C1", CID).

> I don't think we compete with them [MJIB] in digital forensics…I still believe the most important thing [for the police] is to arrest money mules and seize the stolen cash (Commander "C3", CID)

> Specifically, leadership, clear and separated responsibility, information and resource sharing, and cross-agency collaboration…are attributable factors to this successfully solved case (Chief "C2", Third Precinct, Keelung City Police Bureau)

This case later attracted international attention, especially law enforcement field, not only because the Taiwanese authorities recovered more than 90 percent of the stolen cash (approximately $2.4 out of $2.6 million US dollars) but also because Taiwan is the first state to arrest, prosecute, convict, sentence, and imprison three members of the Cobalt group who has allegedly committed more than a hundred ATM heists globally (Devereux, Wild, & Robinson, 2018; Finkle & Wu, 2017). However, similar incidents continued to occur in other countries because of *a lack of timely international collaboration*. As NPA officers highlighted:

> The suspects came from Russia, Romania, and other East European countries that Taiwan does not have diplomatic relation. Although we reported suspects to Interpol, they don't care much because we are not a member of Interpol. (Chief "C2", Third Precinct, Keelung City Police Bureau)

4.1 Implication in Policing

> After FCB case occurred in July, the same group of criminals committed another case in Romania in September (of the same year). They have committed numerous similar crimes. (Commander "C3", CID)

> Two months after the Taiwanese FCB incident, the same criminal group [Cobalt] used the same technique and committed another ATM attack in Romania. Several bagmen recognized from the FCB case were also involved in that case. There were quite a few similar criminal incidents that have occurred across Europe… they [Europol] are familiar with this type of crime, even have identified a few suspects, but Europol has not arrested anyone [at the time of interview] because of insufficient evidence…we shared the investigation process, computer forensic results and other case related reports with Europol, our experience intrigued them on case follow up… (Supervisor "C4", CID)

Nearly 2 years after the clearance of FCB case, Europol, in collaboration with several countries' law enforcement force, arrested the hacker in Spain in March of 2018. Even though Taiwan is a state that has not been officially recognized by many countries, political institutions, and international forums, the positive outcome of the FCB case highlights the competency and professionalism of Taiwanese law enforcement in dealing with transnational crime and cyber investigations. The FCB case also demonstrates Taiwanese authorities' capacity to working with international allies in fighting economic-driven cybercrime. As police officers explained:

> We are not a member of Interpol, so we have to rely on our international allies to receive information. We have tried to be a member of Interpol without success…However, Interpol is very interested in ATM hacking cases. (Commander "L1", CID)

> …we report the [FCB] case to the Interpol because such type of crimes usually occurred in Europe, however, we have insightful details. Interpol are very eager to cooperate, although Taiwan is not a member…I do not perceive the constraints of non-Interpol membership regarding information sharing that we used to have…because of FCB case, Europol invited us to meet with them three times to exchange anti-cybercrime experience in Taiwan, and they also share the European experience… (Commander "C3", CID)

Preventing or even fighting borderless cybercrime still poses challenges to modern societies because this emerged type of crime can occur beyond the physical constraints and human-made barriers. While the police are largely organized and restricted by traditionally defined jurisdictions, criminals have been organized to navigate illegal or illegitimate opportunities in the cyberspace. Such a revolving social-technical gap (Huang & Wang, 2009) and characteristics of the cyberspace would demand new investigative tools and coping strategies. More non-traditional ways of thinking, prosecutorial tools, and collaborations across agencies would be routine requirement when facing challenges of cybercrime that target homeland. Both Taiwanese citizens and law enforcement agencies express their concerns about cybercrime and faced challenges:

> After years of reporting social news…I personally think that cybercrime, including the FCB case, is difficult to prevent (Journalist "A1")

> …we [police] presented the current case [FCB case] and investigation information along with digital forensics evidence to law enforcement agencies in the United States, Thailand,

South Korea, Europe etc… afterwards, we received requests for international investigative cooperation from Mainland China…and the Netherlands…. (Supervisor "C1", CID)

International corporations, indeed, may face political pressure on the 'one China policy' from many states…but for cybercrime this might be a different issue…[for example] Mainland China, a communist society, and America have not yet found a good way to discuss criminal cases… when they [U.S.] conducted cybercrime investigations, they found many [Chinese] hackers use the proxy servers in Taiwan as a path of attack and want us [Taiwan] to help figure out what happened. We are on a very unique position. (Commander "C3", CID)

Despite the fact that Taiwanese authorities successfully solved the FCB case, technically, we have no clue as to who the real hacker behind this incident was… still, we are closer to identifying and apprehending more members of the Cobalt group than any other country… more importantly, we should jump out of the box of traditional crime investigation because cybercrime happened in a virtual space with anonymity and no boundaries. (Special Agent "S")

The experience of the Taiwanese FCB case offers practical lessons for similar foreseeable cybercrimes (see Volz, 2018), as well as demonstrates the nature of relations between law enforcement agencies. Details of the modus operandi and investigation provided by the investigating agents highlight the risks of cyber victimization, particularly how contemporary criminals take advantage of the Internet to "rob" financial institutions in the international community (Sancho, Huq, & Michenzi, 2017). Moreover, given its geopolitical position in West Pacific region, Taiwan is at the forefront between democratic and communist regimes and may be targeted by more cyberattacks. With the largest number of Internet users in the world, the current one-party Chinese government maintains tight control over telecommunication infrastructure and related industry for the nature of information distribution (Liang & Lu, 2010). The Chinese Communist Party (CCP) is highly interested in systematically enforcing Internet censorship. Regardless Internet users are behind the "Great Firewall of China" and overseas, policing Chinese citizens' speech in the cyberspace is an ongoing process, including those popular platforms like WeChat. As one of officers suggests:

Because of China, especially the chair [at the time of interview] is a Chinese, Taiwan has not been able to join Interpol…however, we never stop exchanging information [of criminals] with the police in China…International community is very interested in Taiwan's ability in terms of investigating cybercrime. Western countries recognize our [ability in] cyber forensics and Taiwan's international status because we operate democracy while China is a communist country… It is difficult for U.S. to communicate with and understand China, and some investigations of cybercrime have to route through Taiwan…China's cyber investigation is mysterious [to Western countries] because they have a lot of Internet military, and the scale is huge…North Korea also has a lot of Internet military. There are many usages of Internet military… (Commander "C3, CID)

4.2 Implication in Theory

In early development of cyber criminology, the variation of crime online can be considered as traditional crime "migrated" from the physical space to the virtual space. Internet services like email was used as a new mean to supplement or substitute traditional means like USPS mail and telephone in order to commit traditional crimes like fraud. Mere difference of the medium of criminal means leads to very similar patterns and prevention approaches of cybercrime. From this perspective, some had argued that cybercrimes were "old wine in new bottles." Accompanied with the development of technology, the type of misuse or abuse of the Internet might have gone beyond imagination from traditional frameworks (Wall, 1998), while the essential elements of crime remain regardless of means or targets (Grabosky, 2001).

Despite the above arguments and ongoing debates, scholars have attempted to apply existing theoretical frameworks to explain an array of cybercrimes. Related theoretical and empirical literature gradually emerge. Among them, routine activity theory probably has been applied most frequently to explain varied incidents in the arena of cybercrime (Holt & Bossler, 2016). Originally, Cohen and Felson's (1979) proposed routine activity theory to understand the patterns of upward-trending predatory crimes in the changing social context accompanied with economic transformation in 1950s and 1960s. For a crime to occur, Cohen and Felson theorized three core elements that must converge at the same time and location: a motivated offender, a suitable target, and the absence of capable guardian. This theory of crime does not intend to understand an offender's motivation or offer a psychological explanation of criminal behaviors. Rather, the primary concern of the theory is on the characteristics of crime where "the spatio-temporal organization of social activities helps people to translate their criminal inclinations into action" (Cohen & Felson, 1979, p. 589). Offenses become a feasible or appealing alternative in social situations structured by the legitimate daily routines in which properties and/or people appear to be attractive targets for those who are motivated.

The three essential elements—the predispositions for committing offenses, target suitability derived from routine legitimate activities, and the extent of inadequate protection and ineffective supervision provided by guardians—constructs the three pillars of a given crime. Theoretically speaking, taking off any one of the three pillars would eliminate predatory crime from occurring, which offers many implications in victimization and crime prevention. An increasing opportunity of enjoying rewards obtained from criminal activities can escalate the propensity for predatory violations. A suitable target can be a person, an object, or a place in routine activity theory, and an assessment of the suitability of target depends on cumulatively weighted factors (e.g. visibility, value, accessibility). In general, a suitable target is subjectively assessed by potential offenders who believe the rewards of illegal activities would outweigh the potential punishment and negative consequences, which turn into gains from taking the action.

Routine activities theory has been applied to explain a wide range of crimes in the physical space (e.g., robbery, theft, larceny, burglary, fraud, vandalism, aggravated assault) with lots of empirical support. With the intention of not reinventing the wheel, RAT has also been employed as the theoretical framework to explain emerged cybercrime and victimization facilitated or commissioned in the cyberspace, and the three elements of crime remain valid in understanding the ecological niche of cybercrime (Grabosky, 2001; Leukfeldt & Yar, 2016). A growing body of literature has evidenced the capacity of RAT in terms of understanding contemporary cybercrime and online victimization (Choi & Lee, 2017; Holt & Bossler, 2013; Perkins, Howell, Dodge, Burruss, & Maimon, 2020; Pratt, Holtfreter, & Reisig, 2010), despite the fact that RAT was originally proposed to theorize predatory crimes in physical space. The three key elements—motivated offenders, suitable targets, and the absence of capable guardians—remain valid in explaining cyber criminality that may have specific constrains about cyber accessibility associated with subjects, approaches, time and location.

4.2.1 Motivated Offenders

Cohen and Felson's (1979) theoretical perspective considering physical space is filled with offenders, and these offenders are likely to be motivated by opportunities emerged in the cyberspace and characteristics of the Internet. It is largely agreed that there are motivated offenders out there seeking opportunities to commit crimes, including the cyberspace. The nature of cyberspace allows potential offenders to approach attractive targets in a virtual world that is not constrained by physical proximity. More importantly, three elements of crime—offenders, victims, guardians—are all in digital form in the cyberspace. Thus, motivated offenders can be virtually close to valuable targets, people or properties, that are not adequately guarded. The digital form of victims is literally the information/data in the cyberspace (Eck & Clarke, 2003). Conceptually, properties of RAT can be identified in the cyberspace that are congruent with the physical space (Yar, 2005).

To initiate a hacking attack, offenders might linger in cyberspace waiting for any infected tools to be "clicked" by online users in order to launch the attack. The valuation of targets and calculation of cost and benefit is timed to fit the rhythm of cyberspace. Before using malware to open the "backdoor" of a computer or an information system, the timing of developing or purchasing the malicious software and disseminating the malware is part of the preparation work. Those malware or bogus phishing websites do not "just happen to be there." The time and efforts devoted on these preparations evidence offenders' malicious intention to infect computing devices or network equipment, although offenders are motivated for different reasons.

Social engineering remains the most often used method by hackers to take the initial step of cyberattacks (Mitnick & Simon, 2001), and phishing, as well as "smishing" and "vishing" depends on the tools abused, are techniques to carry out deceptive intentions. Computer viruses, worms, Trojan horses, ransomware, spyware, to name a few are like "screwdrivers" in hackers' toolbox. To maximize the exposure of prospective victims, offenders would keep their contagious and malicious files active in order to circulate in any cyber location (e.g. social media sites, bogus web pages, online advertisement, chat rooms, portals) and infect as many devices/systems as possible. To deceive potential victims, bogus websites with embedded malware have to constantly change online addresses (before being detected, reported and shut down) (Anti-Phishing Working Group, 2020). In this sense, the variation of online victimization, to some degree, depends on victims' online behavior and awareness of risks. Whether unprotected Internet users are virtually proximate to a perpetrator's programed malware (e.g., computer viruses, worms, Trojan horses, ransomware, spyware, and other malicious codes) is somewhat contingent upon users' decisions (Holt & Bossler, 2013).

Despite online banking is legitimately convenient to customers and cost-saving to financial institutions, empirical studies have shown that online banking and computer use are risk factors for phishing victimization (Hutchings & Hayes, 2009). Internet users who engage in the most online banking are more likely to be attacked by motived offenders even though their computers and network equipment are protected by antivirus software and firewall to some extent. Furthermore, users who engage in computer deviance such as using pirated software and media, visiting pornographic sites and viewing obscene materials many of which mimic "hacker-like" behaviors would increase the chance of being targeted while surfing online (Holt & Bossler, 2009). Above common examples illustrate with just a few "clicks" on the Internet, prospective victims can dispose themselves or be redirected to virtual locations that are in close proximity to cybercriminals (Yar, 2005). Users' online activities with their IP addresses proximate their "cyber locations" and show in-use devices or systems that are potentially vulnerable to online offenders (Ministry of Justice Investigation Bureau, 2019). Although it has been argued that routine activity theory might not directly apply to the structure of cyberspace as it often appears disorganized temporally and spatiality in the virtual environment (Yar, 2005), for a cybercrime to take place studies found that components of routine activities exist (Taylor et al., 2006; Holt & Bossler, 2009, 2013; Hutchings & Hayes, 2009).

4.2.2 Suitable Targets

Suitable targets in cybercrimes can be tangible (e.g., computers, cash, people) and intangible (e.g., data, software, music/movies, cryptocurrency). To what extent the targets are attractive to a predator is contingent upon an array of factors and conditions. An increasing likelihood of economic gain, ego satisfaction, and achievement from the criminal actions would seduce offenders to take the risk and commit an offense. Thus, "valuation of targets" is a crucial factor for cybercrime (Yar, 2005:

419). With a wide array of cyberattack techniques, motivated criminals can commit or commission different cybercrimes, ranging from compromise and damage computer systems, steal personal and organizational data and intellectual properties, stalk and harass internet users, to intervene in online services for trading, selling, exchanging services. It is important to point out that these targets in the cyberspace are informational (intangible) in nature. To criminals, high value and portability are desirable characteristics of tangible targets. From this perspective, targets in the cyberspace are intangible and nearly weightless; online targets are easy to transport, hide, and turn into other valuable assets (e.g., bitcoin). Selecting suitable individuals or organizations in a cyberspace with higher levels of vulnerability is necessary for obtaining a greater likelihood of "gains" with respect to profitable rewards, financial gains or other malicious purposes.

From the perspective of victimization, Internet users with certain characteristics or user behaviors have created opportunities for perpetrators to approach them. Individual characteristics like older age, inadequate account and payment settings, low self-control, and a tendency to engage in remote shopping seem to attract online perpetrators (Holtfreter & Meyers, 2015; Reisig & Holtfreter, 2013). By analyzing British Crime Survey, Reyns (2013) pointed out a list of risk factors of online identity theft victimization in behavioral terms (e.g., spending more time online, using email and instant message, downloading software, shopping online, managing finances and banking online). For consumer fraud victimization online, users' socioeconomic backgrounds would affect their online activities, and those who spend more time surfing the net, consuming online and visiting online forums (e.g. Instagram, Facebook, Twitter or other social media sites) are at greater risk of being targeted by fraudsters (Pratt et al., 2010; van Wilsem, 2013). As people are more likely to stay at home during the COVID-19 pandemic, more time have been spent on social media and sharing information about themselves, living space, pets' names, types of car, etc. More information revealed on the social media means more materials for cyber attackers to guess passwords and craft a script of social engineering.

In another example of target suitability, a prospective victim's online personal information such as social media or instant messenger IDs, or e-mail can be sufficient for perpetrators to pursue attacks, however, some relatively private personal information (e.g. photos, videos, sexual orientation, gender, relationship status) could also be valuable to offenders and might make targets more desirable than other targets without these certain traits (Reyns, Henson, & Fisher, 2011). Marcum, Higgins, and Ricketts (2010) revealed that high school students who spend more time in chat rooms and provide more personal or in depth information (e.g. demographic background, school, family status, pictures, emotions, activities, sexual preferences) online are at higher risk of receiving sexual solicitations. This study also indicated that college students who have received unwanted sexually explicit materials were more likely to have posted personal profile and daily life information on social networking and were communicating with people via their electronic devices and the Internet. All of these online activities appear to be related to making oneself a more attractive target to offenders.

4.2.3 Absence of Capable Guardians

Cohen and Felson (1979: 605) argued that a lack of effective social control and punishment mechanisms would result in an increase "in the certainty, celerity and value of rewards to be gained from illegal predatory acts" which may result in more predatory crime taking place." In a similar vein, without capable guardianship in cyberspace, there is an increase of likelihood for illegal gains and the propensity for victimization (Marcum et al., 2010; Reyns et al., 2011). Cyber guardianship ranges widely from informal guardians (e.g. in-house network administrators, ethical private and public computer users) to formal guardians (e.g. firewalls, anti-virus software, IT staff, severity monitors and supervisors). Furthermore, whether the guardian is willing to supervise and intervene when necessary, as well as able to detect potential offenders, is practically important (Reynald, 2010). All of these efforts are critical for deterring potential criminals and controlling and preventing the convergence of motivated offenders and suitable targets in cyberspace (Yar, 2005).

Despite the argument that there is no significant effectiveness in the use of email filters (Hutchings & Hayes, 2009) and physical computer guardianship (Holt & Bossler, 2009), Williams (2016) found that those online users who were less likely to adopt passive physical guardianship measures such as using an email filtering system, installing anti-virus browsing and using only one computer were more likely to be victimized. Moreover, those less likely to be victims of identity theft were those more likely to use avoidance personal guardianship, for instance, spending less time online and doing less shopping and banking online. Another study showed that temporal guardians such as having a friend visible in a place where the Internet is being used and using it in places (e.g. living room, school computer lab) where there is some level of guardianship reduces the likelihood of being victims of receiving online sexually explicit material and receiving online harassment, respectively (Marcum et al., 2010).

Routine risky Internet-using behaviors also include using unguarded networks through connecting to public Wi-Fi hotspots (e.g. airport, subways, coffee shops, bus, restaurants, hotels). To a certain extent, some behavioral habits place individuals at a greater risk of being hacked. Typing sensitive information (e.g. social security number, account numbers, passwords, banking information, credit cards) while connected to a Wi-Fi network without adequate encryptions or security measures allows motivated perpetrators who are in the same time and space (on the same network) to find opportunities to penetrate computers and access personal assets (Reyns, 2013).

In summary, a number of studies have adopted RAT to explain cybercrime across types of victimization and support the concept of the convergence in time and space of motivated offenders, suitable targets and the absence of capable guardians that leads to crimes occurring in cyberspace. Despite some arguments (see Leukfeldt & Yar, 2016; Yar, 2005), empirical studies appear to support the applicability of the routine activity framework in cybercrime. The following section attempts to apply the theoretical framework to ATM hacking, with an aid from the FCB case, and to advance the interpretations of the three elements of crime.

4.2.4 Routine Activity Theory 2.0

There are a few important theoretical implications that FCB case, which is "sampled" from a long series of ATM hackings, can contribute. First, FCB case provides additional supporting evidence of applying a criminological theory to the cyberspace and help understand the virtual criminality. Routine activity theoretical framework emphasizes an interdependent relationship among three elements: the predispositions of committing offenses, valuation of target suitability derived from legitimate routine activities, and the degree of inadequate protection or absence of guardianship, and these three key elements must emerge "in *space* and *time*, involving specific persons and/or objects" (Cohen & Felson, 1979, p. 589). In cyberspace, motivated offenders are not constrained by physical boundaries but instead are "close by" online targets in virtual proximity distance meaning just a few "clicks" away. As an MJIB special agent explains:

> …if we [law enforcement] could not identify a motived offender in the physical environment, even if they have not completely committed a crime yet, imagine how much more difficult it is in cyberspace with a much better anonymous state than in the physical environment. You can imagine that we do have 'invisible' motivated cyber criminals out there… just simply 'a click away' without physical boundaries, distance, and location constraints, they [hackers] are closer to us than you have ever thought when you are on a network… (Special Agent "S", MJIB)

Thus, the existence of motivated offenders in the FCB case is clearly evidenced. Before the FCB case, the Carbanak/Cobalt group had committed more than a hundred of similar cases, victimized dozens of financial institutions internationally, and took enormous financial advantages. Further, the case revealed the pattern of advanced persistent attack (APT) (Kaspersky Lab, 2015; Singer & Friedman, 2014) against carefully selected human targets—certain FCB staff—who are likely to have user privileges and access credentials of the internal networks. Specific ATM model was the valuable target selected by the criminal group who had shown signs of familiarity with financial services software and networks. All these make the criminal motivation undeniable, despite the cyberspace might appear to be temporally and spatially disorganized.

Second, notorious hacker Kevin Mitnick once pointed out that hackers often start with "social engineering" techniques to deceive online users and then use various malware as "tools" to infect computers and information systems, and then open the "backdoor" for hackers to creep in (Mitnick & Simon, 2001). An investigator in the FCB explains:

> …investigation showed that one alleged explanation [for the FCB case] is the hackers infiltrated a voice recording system in London through 'spear phishing' against an administrator who holds specific credential in the first place… this is a very common 'social

engineering' that hackers would use to trick individuals into clicking on something they should not click like a hyperlink, an image, an ad…it is true that companies may continue to upgrade their institutional cyber defense system, yet how to prevent 'human error' is much harder. Many cases have shown that any internal system can be easily breached by someone's mistakes. This illustrates why educating employees on cybersecurity is critical for preventing the exploitation of their accounts by hackers. (Special Agent "S", MJIB)

In other words, "phishing" is usually an instrumental part of social engineering allowing hackers to reach potential victims and set up further cyberattacks (Soudijn & Zegers, 2012). Some Internet users are at a greater risk of being targeted because of their routine online behaviors; people who spend more time on online social interactions (e.g., online forums, chat rooms, social media) are more likely to receive unwanted sexual solicitations and interpersonal violence (Marcum et al., 2010; van Wilsem, 2013). In the FCB case, the London branch administrator, who was *specifically* selected by the cyber criminals, clicked a phishing email sent by the Carbanak/Cobalt group which resulted in the subsequent infiltration of the FCB network (Finkle & Wu, 2017).

Third, according to Cohen and Felson (1979, p. 589), "the spatio-temporal organization of [cyber] social activities helps people to translate their criminal inclinations into action," and, on top of that, cyberspace offers social interactions with anonymity. Spatial properties in the virtual environment could be partially identified and be congruent with physical space. For example, to initiate a hack attack, offenders might loiter in cyberspace waiting for any infected tools (e.g., computer viruses, worms, Trojan horses, ransomware, spyware) to be "clicked" by online users in order to penetrate the information system for further financial advantages (Holt & Bossler, 2013; Mitnick & Simon, 2001). Given that user's IP addresses might signal their "cyber locations" along with exposing their in-use devices or information systems to online perpetrators, this act creates an offender-victim interaction which serves as a proxy of the physical space assumed in routine activity theory (Reyns et al., 2011).

In the FCB case, suitable targets were not limited to stereotypical victims; instead, the focus was on ATMs. The Carbanak/Cobalt group targeted a specific ATM model (PC 1500XE) with security-related vulnerabilities that have been identified by the industry. An increased opportunity of enjoying the rewards obtained from illegal activities would enhance the propensity for predatory violations. For cyber offenders, an increased likelihood of "gain" (e.g. profit, value, ego satisfaction and achievement) would be particularly true in the current case, when vulnerabilities of a specific ATM model were known and remote control was possible. As an investigator relates,

This is a totally rational and well calculated operation…if they have done it before and have not been caught [by the police], it is easy for them to replicate the modus operandi here [in Taiwan]…once you know you can easily remote control ATMs to spit out cash in a few seconds, this is definitely easy money, a very lucrative gain. (Special Agent "S", MJIB)

After the hackers conducted a worldwide search to locate the vulnerable ATM model, Taiwan was targeted by the Carbanak/Cobalt group for a cyber attack as were 13 other European countries (Finkle & Wu, 2017). As demonstrated here, prospective cyber criminals exploit the vulnerability of a cyber security defense system, including machines and humans, and wait for opportunities to further penetrate the system that can be created by negligent service provisions. Although the vulnerability of the ATM model was well-known with in the bank industry, it remains empirically unknown that how many financial institutions take preventative steps as remedy actions.

In other words, individual vulnerabilities would be an "infected spot." With Internet accessibility, the penetration is facilitated from one spot to the other user's private accounts, business servers, and institutions' computer centers or other information systems connected to either the Intranet or Internet. Therefore, capable guardianship does not only depend on formal guardians (e.g. anti-malware software) but also relies on levels of person-based cybersecurity awareness (Leukfeldt, 2014). As the investigator in FCB case, agent "S" relates:

> From a cybersecurity perspective, reducing employees' online risky behaviors is perhaps harder to do than to improve a system of firewalls for the physical environment. This is because while you can just 'upgrade' the security system, say within twenty four hours, you cannot simply change a user's mindset and patterns of online behavior within one day… and for many of us, we think 'oh, I would not be the unlucky one being picked on by hackers', 'They [hackers] can gain nothing from me', or 'I never watch pornography online, I am very careful about this'…there are so many reasons that we don't take this [cyber security] seriously… the truth is you never know when you may be tricked or what mistake you might make at the moment creating a door allowing hackers in [your information system]…. hence, applying the doctrine of cannikin law, we must improve the weakest security spot in order to elevate the magnitude of cyber guardianship. (Special Agent "S", MJIB)

In sum, when discussing routine activity theory, physical and virtual environments appear to be two different spaces under the perception of temporal and spatial disorganization (Yar, 2005), and the FCB case study indicates that they are interrelated. There are spatial properties in the virtual world that can be identified and considered partially congruent with physical space. The FCB case offers theoretical insight that motivated offenders (e.g., hackers online and bagmen on site) and targeted ATMs (e.g., physical locations and online IP addresses) have to be congruent in both physical space and virtual space at the same time without capable guardians (e.g., citizens and the police on site, information security mechanism online) in order to complete a digital robbery through hacking. To prepare and initiate a cyber attack, offenders spread prepared malware and loiter in cyberspace waiting for any infected tools (e.g., computer viruses, worms, Trojan horses, ransomware, spyware) to be triggered by online users in order to penetrate the information system for further financial advantages (Holt & Bossler, 2013; Mitnick & Simon, 2001). Just like traditional fraudsters would prepare and distribute "baits" like fraudulent mails in physical space, the criminal scenario of ATM hacking also relies on pre-incident preparation to allow hackers obtaining access credentials and then install malware on the ATMs. However, to successfully complete a high-tech "bank robbery", the malware execution on the ATMs has to be perfectly timed with the bagmen standing by the machines to pick up the cash.

Prior studies with a narrower scope of guardians and with a focus on human elements (e.g., emphasized an order of responsibility for human guardians) (Felson, 1995) would struggle with the concept of guardianship in cyberspace (Hollis, Felson, & Welsh, 2013). While such studies did not support the relationship between person-based guardianship (e.g., living arrangements) and the likelihood of cyber-victimization (Henson, Reyns, & Fisher, 2016), the current study echoes later works that broaden the conceptual definition of guardianship (e.g., target hardening) to enable it to apply to cybercrime (Ngo & Paternoster, 2011; Reyns et al., 2011) and the role played by users in cyber security (Leukfeldt, 2014). Consistent with these newer studies, the FCB case implies that guardianship in terms of target hardening such as anti-malware and physical security systems does not prevent person-based victimizations that often start with social engineering (Holt & Bossler, 2016; Mitnick & Simon, 2001). Person-based guardianship remains valid in physical space, but neither the theoretical framework can be simply adopted in the virtual space without updating conceptual scope nor the nature of user behaviors in the cyberspace can be ignored. It is true that institutional and organizational features provide capable formal guardians in both physical space (e.g. physical security defense systems, security guards) and virtual space (e.g., anti-malware software, firewalls), and the importance of personal capable guardianship (e.g., phishing awareness) is critical in reducing the harm caused by cybercriminals.

4.3 Conclusion

A series of transnational ATM hackings have shown that modern computer capacity and information technology has enabled criminals to commit increasingly sophisticated crimes in the cyberspace. Actually, the successfully solved FCB case evidences cybercriminals cannot afford to not be perfectionists and leave any "digital footprint." While cybercriminals have abused the Internet to a great extent and some nations/states have "weaponized" the Internet to suppress internal opponents or attack other regimes, developing countries represent a group of vulnerable targets because of an imbalance between structural demands of information technology and institutional capacity of cyber security (Antonescu & Birau, 2015). The magnitude, scope, speed, and impact of cyber threats is constantly evolving. To secure their homeland, law enforcement have to keep updating their investigative capacity in information technology, and the most effective approach is through cross-agency collaborations (Wang et al., 2020). In democratic countries, collaborations between local agencies often require local supports to satisfy the principle of self-governing. For example, the oldest national measure of crime in the U.S.—FBI Uniform Crime Reports—was a result of local law enforcement agencies' voluntary support and participation institutionalized through the *International Association of Chiefs of Police* (IACP).

However, disincentives of collaborations, including inter-agency and intra-agency "turf jealousies," remain in practice. In the FCB case, local police are more likely to mention their working relation with other law enforcement agencies than MJIB. Similarly, compared with the FBI, federal law enforcement agencies like the Bureau of Alcohol, Tobacco, Firearms, and Explosives (ATF) appears to have a better working relationship with local police. It is worth noting that both MJIB and FBI have prioritized mission of fighting local corruption and thus often investigating police departments. In addition, when law enforcement agencies are function to supplement rather than overlap, collaborations are more likely to form. Traditional bureaucratic boundaries and competition in policing assignments, resources (Stewart, 2011), and organizational culture (Cohen, 2017) are barriers of collaborative relationship among national-local law enforcement agencies.

FBI has warmed "a blending of threats, such as nation state adversaries using criminal actors as proxies to mask their activities" (Wallace, 2020). Whether there is a nation/state actively facilitates or passively ignores criminal groups' highly intelligent ATM hackings may remain unknown forever, the authorities should enhance cyber security at different levels as part of their homeland security strategy. Also, criminological theories can help understand virtual criminality and offer policy and pragmatic implications. Additionally, rigorous measures of cyber security would involve law enforcement and public entities, citizens, and private industries.

Practically, phishing remains one of the top ways hackers gain initial entry into a network, and it is believed to be the case for future cyberattacks against financial institutions. Effective phishing attacks usually use compelling lures and bait employees, and spear phishing campaigns are seen more frequently. The spread of COVID-19 has brought many uncertainties to people in the world, and new phishing scams have used the pandemic to trick frazzled victims into clicking on malicious hyperlinks that look like urgent coronavirus guidelines from the government or updated statistics of infections/deaths. For a recent example, UK faced COVID-19 themed phishing attacks peaked when the US announced a travel ban to Europe and when Prime Minister Boris Johnson was moved to intensive care. Other examples include offering working-from-home job opportunities that appear to be very appealing, especially to people who lost jobs because of the outbreak. Furthermore, with millions of people working from home during COVID-19 pandemic, more vulnerabilities have been unwillingly introduced to institutions' cybersecurity. To any institutions, monitoring whether employees follow security protocols beyond the office space is more challenging. On top of that, family members and home environment often distract work-from-home employees from operating in full capacity and be altered with phishing attacks. The current tragedy of COVID-19 pandemic (The New England Journal of Medicine, 2020) proves that there is no shortage of creativity in the cybercrime. With that said, ATM hacking is likely to continue, and "native" digital robbery without collecting cash in the physical space may become more preferable to cyber criminals.

References

Anti-Phishing Working Group. (2020). Phishing Attack Trends Report – 2Q.

Antonescu, M., & Birau, R. (2015). Financial and non-financial implications of cybercrimes in emerging countries. *Procedia Economics and Finance, 32*, 618–621.

Cao, L., Huang, L., & Sun, I. (2014). *Policing in Taiwan: From authoritarianism to democracy*. London, UK: Routledge.

Choi, K.-S., & Lee, J. R. (2017). Theoretical analysis of cyber-interpersonal violence victimization and offending using cyber-routine activities theory. *Computers in Human Behavior, 73*, 394–402.

Cohen, G. (2017). Cultural fragmentation as a barrier to interagency collaboration: A qualitative examination of Texas law enforcement officers' perceptions. *American Review of Public Administration, 48*(8), 886–901.

Cohen, L. E., & Felson, M. (1979). Social change and crime rate trends: Routine activity approach. *American Sociological Review, 44*(4), 588–608.

Devereux, C., Wild, F. & Robinson, E. (2018, June 25). The biggest digital heist in history isn't over yet. Retrieved October 10, 2020 from https://www.bloomberg.com/news/features/2018-06-25/the-biggest-digital-heist-in-history-isn-t-over-yet

Eck, J. E., & Clarke, R. V. (2003). Classifying common police problems: A routine activity approach. *Crime Prevention Studies, 16*, 7–39.

Europol. (March 26, 2018). *Mastermind behind Euro 1 billion cyber bank robbery arrested in Spain*. Retrieved October 13, 2020, from http://www.europol.europa.eu/newsroom/news/mastermind-behind-eur-1-billion-cyber-bank-robbery-arrested-in-spain

Felson, M. (1995). Those who discourage crime. In J. E. Eck & D. Weisburd (Eds.), *Crime and place: Crime prevention studies* (Vol. 4, pp. 53–66). Monsey, NY: Criminal Justice Press.

Finkle, J., & Wu, J. R. (2017, January 4). Taiwan ATM heist linked to European hacking spree: Security firm. *Reuters*. Retrieved October 10, 2020, from https://www.reuters.com/article/us-taiwan-cyber-atms/taiwan-atm-heist-linked-to-european-hacking-spree-security-firm-idUSKBN14P0CX

Geller, W. A., & Morris, N. (1992). Relations between federal and local police. In M. Tonry & N. Morris (Eds.), *Modern policing* (pp. 231–348). Chicago, IL: University of Chicago Press.

Grabosky, P. N. (2001). Virtual criminality: Old wine in new bottles? *Social and Legal Studies, 10*, 243–249.

Henson, B., Reyns, B. W., & Fisher, B. S. (2016). Cybercrime victimization. In C. A. Cuevas & C. M. Rennison (Eds.), *The Wiley handbook on the psychology of violence* (pp. 555–570). Wiley Blackwell.

Hollis, M. E., Felson, M., & Welsh, B. C. (2013). The capable guardian in routine activities theory: A theoretical and conceptual reappraisal. *Crime Prevention and Community Safety, 15*, 65–79.

Holt, T. J., & Bossler, A. M. (2009). Examining the applicability of lifestyle-routine activities theory for cybercrime victimization. *Deviant Behavior, 30*, 1–25.

Holt, T. J., & Bossler, A. M. (2013). Examining the relationship between routine activities and malware infection indicators. *Journal of Contemporary Criminal Justice, 29*(4), 420–436.

Holt, T. J., & Bossler, A. M. (2016). *Cybercrime in progress: Theory and prevention of technology-enabled offenses*. New York: Routledge.

Holtfreter, K., & Meyers, T. J. (2015). Challenges for cybercrime theory, research, and policy. In G. C. Lajeunessehe (Ed.), *Norwich review of international and transnational crime* (pp. 54–66). Norwich, VT: The Program of International and Transnational Crime.

Huang, W., & Wang, S.-Y. K. (2009). Emerging cybercrime variants in the socio technical space. In B. Whitworth & A. de Moor (Eds.), *Handbook of research on socio-technical design and social networking systems* (pp. 209–220). IGI Global: Hershey, PA.

Hutchings, A., & Hayes, H. (2009). Routine activity theory and phishing victimization: Who got caught in the 'net'? *Current Issues in Criminal Justice, 20*, 432–451.

James, S., & Warren, I. (2010). Australian police responses to transnational crime and terrorism. In J. A. Eterno & D. K. Das (Eds.), *Police practices in global perspective* (pp. 207–224). Rowman & Littlefield Publishers, Inc..

Kaspersky Lab. (2015). Carbanak APT: The great Bank robbery.

Leukfeldt, E. R. (2014). Phishing for suitable targets in the Netherlands: Routine activity theory and phishing victimization. *Cyberpsychology, Behavior and Social Networking, 17*(8), 551–555.

Leukfeldt, E. R., & Yar, M. (2016). Applying routine activity theory to cybercrime: A theoretical and empirical analysis. *Deviant Behavior, 37*(3), 263–280.

Liang, B., & Lu, H. (2010). Internet development, censorship, and cyber crimes in China. *Journal of Contemporary Criminal Justice, 26*(1), 103–120.

Marcum, C. D., Higgins, G. E., & Ricketts, M. L. (2010). Potential factors of online victimization of youth: An examination of adolescent online behaviors utilizing routine activity theory. *Deviant Behavior, 31*(5), 381–410.

Ministry of Justice Investigation Bureau. (2019, May 16). *A brief of "First Commercial Bank ATM Heist" investigated by MJIB*. Retrieved October 13, 2020, from https://www.mjib.gov.tw/EditPage/?PageID=ee95cdc2-ec2f-4c2f-be44-50e09a173ddb

Mitchell, G. E., O'Leary, R., & Gerard, C. (2015). Collaboration and performance: Perspectives from public managers and NGO leaders. *Public Performance and Management Review, 38*, 684–716.

Mitnick, K. D., & Simon, W. L. (2001). *The art of deception: Controlling the human element of security*. New York: John Wiley & Sons.

Ngo, F. T., & Paternoster, R. (2011). Cybercrime victimization: An examination of individual and situational level factors. *International Journal of Cyber Criminology, 5*, 773–793.

Perkins, R. C., Howell, C. J., Dodge, C. E., Burruss, G. W., & Maimon, D. (2020). Malicious spam distribution: A routine activities approach. *Deviant Behavior*. https://doi.org/10.1080/01639625.2020.1794269.

Pratt, T. C., Holtfreter, K., & Reisig, M. D. (2010). Routine online activity and internet fraud targeting: Extending the generality of routine activity theory. *Journal of Research in Crime and Delinquency, 47*, 267–296.

Reisig, M. D., & Holtfreter, K. (2013). Shopping fraud victimization among the elderly. *Journal of Financial Crime, 20*, 324–337.

Reynald, D. M. (2010). Guardians on guardianship: Factors affecting the willingness to monitor, the ability to detect potential offenders and the willingness to intervene. *Journal of Research in Crime & Delinquency, 47*, 358–390.

Reyns, B. W. (2013). Online routines and identity theft victimization: Further expanding routine activity theory beyond direct-contact offenses. *Journal of Research in Crime and Delinquency, 50*, 216–238.

Reyns, B. W., Henson, B., & Fisher, B. S. (2011). Being pursued online: Applying cyberlifestyle-routine activities theory to cyberstalking victimization. *Criminal Justice and Behavior, 38*(11), 1149–1169.

Sancho, D., Huq, N., & Michenzi, M. (2017). *Cashing in on ATM malware: A comprehensive look at various attack types*. Retrieved October 10, 2020, from https://documents.trendmicro.com/assets/white_papers/wp-cashing-in-on-atm-malware.pdf

Singer, P. W., & Friedman, A. (2014). *Cybersecurity and cyberwar: What everyone needs to know*. New York: Oxford University Press.

Soudijn, M. R. J., & Zegers, B. C. H. T. (2012). Cybercrime and virtual offender convergence settings. *Trends in Organized Crime, 15*, 111–129.

Stewart, D. M. (2011). Collaboration between federal and local law enforcement: An examination of Texas police chiefs' perceptions. *Police Quarterly, 14*(4), 407–430.

Sunshine, J., & Tyler, T. R. (2003). The role of procedural justice and legitimacy in shaping public support for policing. *Law & Society Review, 37*(3), 513–547.

Taipei District Prosecutors Office. (2017). *Top 10 financial fraud investment records*. Taipei, Taiwan: Taipei District Prosecutors Office.

References

Taylor, R. W., Fritsch, E. J., Liederbach, J., & Holt, T. J. (2011). *Digital crime and digital terrorism*. Upper Saddle River, NJ: Pearson Prentice Hall.

The New England Journal of Medicine. (2020). Dying in a Leadership Vacuum. Retrieved October 10, 2020, from https://www.nejm.org/doi/full/10.1056/NEJMe2029812?query=featured_home

Tyler, T. (1990). *Why people obey the law*. New Haven, CT: Yale University Press.

van Wilsem, J. (2013). Bought it, but never got it: Assessing risk factors for online consumer fraud victimization. *European Sociological Review, 29*(2), 168–178.

Volz, D. (2018, January 29). "Jackpotting" hackers steal over $1 million from ATMs across U.S.: Secret Service. *Reuters*. Retrieved October 10, 2020, from https://www.reuters.com/article/us-usa-cyber-atm/jackpotting-hackers-steal-over-1-million-from-atms-across-u-s-secret-service-idUSKBN1FI2QF

Wall, D. (1998). Catching cybercriminals: Policing the internet. *International Review of Law, Computers & Technology, 12*, 201–218.

Wallace, C. E. (2020, March 4). Dangerous Partners: *Big Tech and Beijing*. Deputy Assistant Director, Cyber Division, Federal Bureau of Investigation. Statement before the Senate Judiciary Committee, Subcommittee on Crime and Terrorism. Retrieved from https://www.fbi.gov/news/testimony/dangerous-partners-big-tech-and-beijing

Wang, S.-Y. K., Hsieh, M.-L., Chang, C., Jiang, P.-S., & Dallier, D. (2020). Collaboration between law enforcement agencies in combating cybercrime. *International Journal of Offender Therapy and Comparative Criminology*.

Waugh, W. L., & Streib, G. (2006). Collaboration and leadership for effective emergency management. *Public Administration Review, 66*(s1), 131–140.

Williams, M. L. (2016). Guardians upon high: An application of routine activities theory to online identity theft in Europe at the country and individual level. *British Journal of Criminology, 56*, 21–48.

Yar, M. (2005). The novelty of cybercrime: An assessment in light of routine activity theory. *European Journal of Criminology, 2*(4), 407–427.

GPSR Compliance

The European Union's (EU) General Product Safety Regulation (GPSR) is a set of rules that requires consumer products to be safe and our obligations to ensure this.

If you have any concerns about our products, you can contact us on

ProductSafety@springernature.com

In case Publisher is established outside the EU, the EU authorized representative is:

Springer Nature Customer Service Center GmbH
Europaplatz 3
69115 Heidelberg, Germany

www.ingramcontent.com/pod-product-compliance
Ingram Content Group UK Ltd.
Pitfield, Milton Keynes, MK11 3LW, UK
UKHW021120240426
470314UK00010B/7